Tom Bridge's
Pie Society

Traditional savoury pies, pasties & puddings from around the British Isles

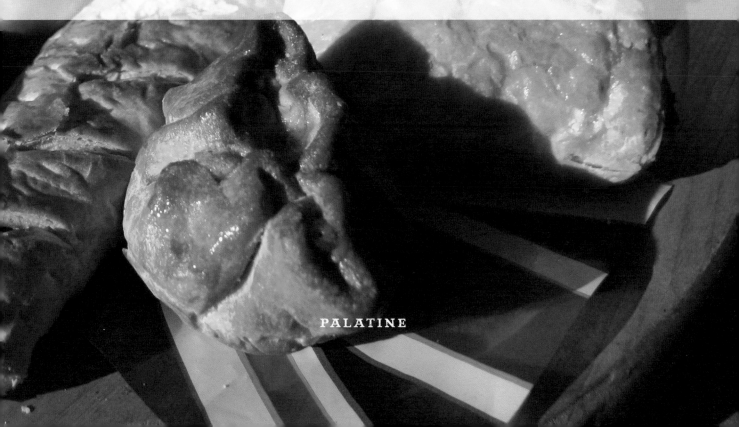

PALATINE

Cooks' notes

All the recipes in this book show both metric and imperial measurements. Conversions are approximate and have been rounded up or down. Choose one set of measurements for a recipe and follow only those; don't mix the two. See the conversion tables at the end of the book for more detail.

Spoon measures are level unless otherwise stated.

Eggs are large size unless otherwise stated, and if you are in a vulnerable health group take care in handling raw eggs and ensure that you avoid dishes containing them.

Oven timings are for fan-assisted ovens. If using a conventional oven increase temperature by about 15°C (1 gas mark), or adjust according to your usual practice with your oven – all ovens vary and you will know your own best. You may wish to use an oven thermometer to test the accuracy of your oven.

All cooking etc. timings are approximate, with a description of colour and texture where appropriate, but readers need to use their own judgement in deciding when a dish is cooked.

Pie Society

Copyright © Tom Bridge, 2010

First edition, 2010

Published by Palatine Books,
an imprint of Carnegie Publishing Ltd
Carnegie House,
Chatsworth Road,
Lancaster, LA1 4SL
www.carnegiepublishing.com

ISBN 978-1-874181-68-2

Designed and typeset by Carnegie Book Production
Printed and bound in the UK by Information Press, Oxford

Pie Society would not be complete without the inclusion of just a few of the many British producers who have made pies their passion. It wouldn't have been possible or desirable to include all of them – this is a recipe book after all! – so what you will find is a small selection from across the UK of different types of pie makers, from artisan to large scale, just to give a flavour. There are loads of equally good companies we haven't been able to include and, when you're not baking your own little beauties, we'd encourage you to sniff out those local to your area, as well as sampling the huge range on offer via supermarkets.

Contents

Foreword

My love for pies started with my mum and dad making homemade mince and onion plate pies for their pub in Bolton in the 1960s and '70s. I grew up with the unbeatable aroma of baking pastry encasing various delicious fillings, and quickly developed a taste for the honest, traditional and economical comfort food that is the savoury British pie.

After training as a chef I was able to follow my passion for food, and pies in particular, soon becoming known for my unique, no-nonsense recipes. This led to some wonderful times working freelance for various food companies, creating new pies for their ranges. I worked with Derek Warburton, of Warburton's bakers, at his factory, then called Peter Hunts, in Farnworth, Lancashire. Then I helped to create a Mrs Beeton range for Ginsters, going on to work for various other well-known manufacturers, such as Pukka Pies, who now sponsor so many sporting events, and Dickinson & Morris, makers of the famous Melton Mowbray pork pie. 25 years on I am still a man obsessed, still trying to make pies even tastier and being ever more creative with fillings and designs!

The original seed of an idea for this book was sown 18 years ago at our cottage in Newburgh, Lancashire, when my wife Jayne and I invited friends for one of our bi-monthly dinners. While relaxing with pleasantly full stomachs after the meal we decided that we would get together in the week before Christmas and enjoy a pie-themed meal. It was agreed that the girls would go off shopping and have a posh lunch, while my friends Peter Vickers, Hubert Lowry and I would enjoy ourselves making various pies for the festive season. Peter and Hubert were not in the catering trade, but did enjoy pie-making, so it fell to me to be the cookery teacher. To maximise our enjoyment during these 'classes', and in payment for my services, the lads brought along a bottle of superb quality single malt whisky (no change from £50 each, if you please!), which we cracked open as soon as we began cooking.

After about 4 hours of really hard work, baking and sweating in a cottage kitchen, enduring the hardship of tippling fabulous single malt, our loving wives returned to be presented with our festive pie of local game blended with cranberries and vintage port in a very crisp water-paste crust. A tremendous time was had by all, the pre-Christmas gathering was established as an annual event, and the notion of a book called 'Pie Society' was born. In the years since our inaugural meeting, I have been fortunate enough to continue to enjoy a very varied and interesting career as a chef, championing good food, researching food history and inventing realistic recipes which use top-quality ingredients, locally sourced wherever possible. And, much to my enormous delight, I have been able to devote many happy hours to the great British pie, its history, folklore and recipes.

Tom Bridge

Introduction

The British have been eating meat pies for over 600 years, and a peek into any well-stocked butcher's shop or delicatessen shows that we mean to continue. In the North of England, where I am from, pies really are a big part of life, and of our history – in fact in many ways they even define the northerner, as Stuart Maconie maintains in *Pies and prejudice: in search of the North*. But, important though they are in this one part of Britain, pies are far from exclusive to it. Traditional favourites can be found on high streets the length and breadth of the country, and every region has its speciality, often made by old-fashioned, small-scale pie factories. In recent years, however, pies have also been part of a general resurgence of interest in British food, albeit often 'poshed-up' versions. There is nothing wrong with posh pies, of course, but this book is dedicated to the more old-fashioned, honest, cookable-at-home pies, from across the British Isles – admittedly with the odd silly one thrown in to indulge my sense of culinary adventure!

Flights of fancy aside, in many ways a pie is food at its simplest, and you can rustle one up very quickly if you keep it simple. However, twenty-first-century pie-making can – and arguably should – require a bit of effort, not so much in the construction as in the ingredients. We should look for the finest ingredients, grown nearby whenever available, and work hard to ensure that no artificial stuff whatsoever is allowed to creep in. In mass production many pie-making factories will use undesirable additives; not I, and not the companies I mention in this book. My guiding principle has always been that all the food we make, whether at home or on a bigger scale, should be wholesome, tasty and unadulterated.

Across the UK we have flourishing farmers' markets, often specialising in both local produce and regional specialities from further afield. On offer to the buyer prepared to spend just a little time looking beyond the shelves of the supermarkets are fine-quality meat, poultry, game, cheeses, fruit and vegetables, much of it emanating from the lush, rain-drenched landscape that our oft-cursed (but actually truly wonderful) climate produces. So whether you live in Land's End, Birmingham or John o' Groats, there is always something on a market stall, in a farm shop or in the greengrocer's round the corner that will taste great wrapped in pastry.

Pie Society

Ingredients: finest fillings, proper pastry, lovely recipes, added cooks & celebrities past & present, selected producers, foodie facts & historical nuggets, tips & suggestions, sauces, sides & seasonings.

Method: Mix all ingredients in any kitchen, stir well, add alcohol as required, then relax and have fun while you cook up a great British pie!

Ah, pastry! That most basic of comfort foods: filling, simple and cheap. In its many guises it provides the perfect jacket for almost anything, and this book offers a wealth of recipes, variations, tips and suggestions to help you to make the tastiest pies imaginable – and if they look homemade, imperfect and rustic, well that's pie for you!

So having sourced the finest fillings and made the best pastry, all we need now are the right natural flavourings. This is such a very important part of this cookbook, and every chef and cook I know puts judicious seasoning at the forefront of their cookery. In all my recipes I only use sea salt and freshly ground pepper, which I recommend you do too; so where I say salt I mean sea salt, and pepper I mean freshly ground. If I was to be marooned on a desert island I would have to have on my wish list sea salt, peppercorns, herbs, spices and a pepper mill. Use of herbs and spices, too, when making pastry, also ensuring that it is not too thick. And finally, use only top quality – preferably homemade – stocks, and the overall result will be a delicious, wonderfully satisfying eating experience.

The '(h)umble pie'

From 1330 onwards many references can be found in Old English and Middle English texts to 'numbles' (or noumbles, nomblys, noubles), the name given to the heart, liver, entrails etc. of animals, especially of deer – what we now call offal or lights. The word numble in turn is derived from the Old French word 'nomble', meaning deer's innards. By the fifteenth century the spelling was usually 'umbles', although different versions of the word co-existed for some time. At that time umbles were used as an ingredient in pies, especially for the poor, although the first recipe for umble pie that I can find in print doesn't appear until the seventeenth century.

Samuel Pepys makes many references to umble pies in his diary, as on 5th July 1662:

> I having some venison given me a day or two ago, and so I had a shoulder roasted, another baked, and the umbles baked in a pie, and all very well done.

and on 8th July 1663:

> Mrs Turner came in and did bring us an Umble-pie hot out of her oven, extraordinarily good.

Recipe for umble pie, 1617

'To make an Umble-pye, or for want of Umbles, to doe it with a Lambes head and Purtenance.

Boyle your meate reasonable tender, take the flesh from the bone, and mince it small with Beefe-suit [suet] and Marrow, with the Liver, Lights, and Heart, a few sweet Hearbes and Currins [currants]. Season it with Pepper, Salt, and Nutmeg: Bake it in a Coffin raised like an Umble pye, and it will eat so like unto Umbles as that you shall hardly by taste discerne it from right Umbles.'

[A New Booke of Cookerie; John Murrell, 1617]

Funnily enough, the adjective humble, meaning 'of lowly rank' or 'having a low opinion of oneself', appears to have developed quite separately from the word umbles. It is easy to see how this similarity in the sounds of the words, and the fact that umble pie was often served to lower-class people, could have given rise to the phrase 'to eat humble pie'. This rather quaint expression, peculiar to Britain, means, of course, to swallow one's pride and make an apology for a mistake.

Ironically, offal pies these days are more likely to be found on trendy restaurant menus than on the street or on a poor man's table, and the high-quality umbles used will probably have cost more than good meat!

THE
YOUNG
WOMAN'S
COMPANION

1813

MRS BEETON'S
HOUSEHOLD
MANAGEMENT

MODEL COOKERY

WARNE'S
MODEL COOKERY

THINGS
IN
ENGLAND

A BOOK OF
REAL
ENGLISH
COOKERY

FLORENCE
WHITE

2nd Impression

853 RECIPES
ILLUSTRATED

MRS A.B.
MARSHALL'S
COOKERY
BOOK

Pie: a potted past

Stroll down any high street in the UK and you will find a bewildering array of savoury pies. Everyday favourites such as pork, steak and kidney, chicken, cheese and onion, meat and potato, are always present, of course, sometimes accompanied by more elaborate versions filled with pheasant, duck or rabbit. In bygone days the list was even longer, with pies commonly containing things like pigeons, doves, quails, peacocks, cranes, and even swans and songbirds.

But where did the idea of a pie originate?

It seems likely that the Romans are to be thanked for bringing what was probably the earliest version of the meat pie to British shores. They sealed meat inside a flour and water paste before cooking, presumably to keep the meat moist. This primitive pastry was used primarily as a container for cooking, rather than being part of the dish, and wasn't designed for consumption. The Romans did, though, also make some pies with an edible crust, usually filled with a game bird.

During the Middle Ages, pie crusts were formed into box-like shapes known as 'coffins', and in old recipes the lifting of the sides of the pastry to form a strong protective container is described as 'raising the coffin' – which is ironic when you consider that current medical evidence tells us that if we eat too much pastry we'll end up in one! Sweet spices, rich fruits, sugar and raisins were often added to the meat fillings inside the 'coffin', while lobster pies, for example, were made with white wine, butter and cream, and chicken pies were covered with bone marrow and ginger. In addition, sugar might be sprinkled on the pie lids, which, for special occasions, could also be coated with a rich icing.

"The pie is a great human discovery which has universal estimation among all civilised eaters"

These sumptuous sweet meat pies were the forerunners of the great Yorkshire Christmas pies, made famous in the eighteenth century when Little Jack Horner stuck his thumb in one and pulled out a plum. Mrs Hanna Glasse, the first woman to produce a best-selling cookery book, passed down a recipe for an enormous Christmas pie. Included in the ingredients were pigeon, partridge, a chicken,

PRODIGIOUS PIES

Bigger again than Mrs Glasse's pie was one described in the *Newcastle Chronicle* of 6 January, 1770, a pie made by a Mrs Dorothy Patterson, housekeeper at Howick:

> It is near nine feet in circumference at bottom, weighs about twelve stones, will take two men to present it to table; it is neatly fitted with a case and four small wheels to facilitate its use to every guest that inclines to partake of its contents at table.

We must also remember the Denby Dale pies, made in the small Yorkshire village since 1788, the custom being that each time the pie is baked it should be larger than the previous one. The last one, baked to celebrate the millennium in 2000, weighed in at a massive 12 tonnes, measured 40 feet long and contained 100 kg of John Smith's best bitter!

A Melton Mowbray pie weighing 29lbs was produced for a special occasion in 1868; it took seven hours to bake! In October 1973 a 30lb pie was produced for the twinning of Melton with Dieppe.

and a whole goose, all carefully boned and placed one inside the other and then put inside a huge turkey. This was placed on a thick pie-crust bottom and surrounded by jointed hares, woodcocks, moor hens, and whatever other wild bird was available. Four pounds of butter were poured into the pie, and a thick crust laid on top. Many of these pies were sent to London as gifts, and the butter sealed and preserved the contents by keeping out the air and prevented the pies from spoiling before they reached their destination. For protection, the raised walls were very thick and often the pies were so large that they were held together by iron bands to withstand the lengthy journey.

The practice of eating meat pies cooked with spices and fruits continued well into the eighteenth century. Sweet veal pies of that period contained layers of marrow above and below the meat, along with candied orange, raisins and brandy. In 1806, the great statesman William Pitt uttered on his death bed one of his more meaty statements: 'I think I could eat one of Bellamy's veal pies.'

In the later eighteenth and the nineteenth centuries, meat pies could be purchased from pie shops, where they could be eaten on the premises or taken away, and by the 1850s they were common fayre in the increasingly popular coffee stalls too. The 'umble' pie was still very much in evidence in

Victorian times, and meat pies were sold all over England by travelling pie men who walked the streets pushing carts or carrying aloft wicker baskets containing their (hopefully!) freshly made wares. They touted for business in pubs and inns and were ever-present at races and fairs – indeed, the nursery rhyme tells us that 'Simple Simon' met one and that 300 years ago a tasty meat pie could be bought for only one penny!

A lovely insight into the life of pie in this period can be found in the 1853 article by Charles Manby Smith reproduced on page 17. Do have a read, it's a fascinating little time capsule!

As is occasionally the case with 'street food' today, there was often a risk in buying from the pie men, so the housewife would be very particular about who she bought from. Some pie men were less than careful, for example not sealing off their pies properly with aspic or butter to prevent them from spoiling, and the conditions in which some of them were made must have been appalling. Needless to say, cases of food poisoning were not uncommon.

It wasn't just the street pie man who could be negligent, however; the makers of a pie made in Denby Dale in 1887 for Queen Victoria's Jubilee had a lot to answer for, too. This enormous pie, claimed at the time to be the largest ever made, was 8 feet in diameter, 2 feet deep and weighed nearly a ton and a half. It contained pork, lamb, beef, mutton, veal, hares, rabbits, potatoes, poultry and over 150 types of game bird – many of which were placed uncooked round the edges of the pie, supposedly so they would cook as the pie was baked.

'THE ROAD TO WIGAN PIE'

Wigan is home to the annual Pie Eating Competition which is held at Harry's Bar on Wallgate in the town centre. The competition has been held since 1992, and in 2007 a vegetarian version was added. Some Wiganers are proud to be called pie-eaters, but the nickname is not thought to be because of their appetite for the delicacy. The name is said to date from the 1926 General Strike when Wigan miners were starved back to work before their counterparts in surrounding towns and were forced to eat humble pie.

Sadly, food hygiene standards fell well short of what we would expect today. A local butcher showcased the huge quantities of meat in his window before it was stewed, and the cooking was done in stages, so that some of the pie components were allowed to stand and cool while others were boiled. Large crowds eagerly anticipated the grand cutting of the pie and jostled to get a good position for the tasting. But, horror of horrors, as the pastry was pierced their nostrils were assaulted by the appalling smell of rotten meat, and not a morsel could be eaten!

By the end of Victoria's reign, the taste for sweetened meat pies had waned, and the much less extravagant savoury pie rose to popularity. In the last 100 years or so many regional pies have passed into history, along with our taste for them. No longer do we routinely hear of Muggety Pie from Gloucestershire, containing the entrails of sheep or calves; Lamb Tail Pie from the Cotswolds; Rook Pie from Somerset, filled with the legs and breasts of skinned rooks; and Stargazy Pie from Cornwall, made with whole herrings or pilchards standing on their tails, heads poking through the pastry, looking up at the heavens.

But a decade into the twenty-first century the traditional British pie is enjoying a huge revival, its popularity no doubt due in part to a general trend towards good, wholesome, sustainable and economical types of food. While some pies have disappeared off the culinary map – and probably a good thing too in many cases! – there are still local varieties of the meat pie in every part of the country. The most famous is probably the pork pie from Melton Mowbray, Leicestershire, where it is still made commercially on a large scale. Carrs, Pukka, Ginster's, Potts, Hollands and Wigan Poole pies, to name but a few, fill the streets and football terraces with the unbeatable aroma of pastry and various luscious fillings; Cornish pasties sell by the bucket-load across the land; and the Scotch pie has successfully been exported to the Sasanachs, and welcomed in a way that Scottish invaders of the past certainly weren't.

From the top of Britain to the very bottom, and from east to west, pies rule. I know I'm a bit of a pie nut, but I also know I am not alone. Whether or not you are already a convert I sincerely hope that the mouthwatering and cookable treats within these pages will lead you into temptation. If pies are a sin, take me to hell!

What has become of the pie man?

A PENNY for a pie! In the records of our individual experience, this is probably the most ancient species of barter – the first gentle and welcome induction to the dry details of commerce, and one eminently calculated to impress upon the infant minds of a trading population the primary principles of exchange, of which a *quid pro quo* forms the universal basis. We had imagined, upon the first view of our subject, that the fabrication and consumption of pies must have been a custom as ancient as cookery itself, and have ranked among the very first achievements of the gastronomic art.

Upon careful investigation, however, we find ourselves to have been mistaken in this idea. We have not been able to discover among the revelations to which the Rosetta stone surrendered a key, any authority for supposing that among all the butlers and bakers of all the Pharaohs, there ever existed one who knew how to prepare a pie for the royal banquet. No; it was reserved for the Greeks, the masters of civilization and the demigods of art, who brought every species of refinement to its highest pitch, to add the invention of pies and pie-crust to the catalogue of their immortal triumphs.

Their *artokreas* (the word passed unchanged into Roman use) was an aggregation of succulent meats baked in a farinaceous crust, probably somewhat resembling in form a venison pasty of the present day, and was the first combination of the kind, so far at least as we know, ever submitted to the appetite of the gourmand. We have no intention of pursuing the history of this great discovery from its first dawn in some Athenian kitchen to its present universal estimation among all civilized eaters.

We must pass the pies of all nations, from the monkey-pie of Central Africa, with the head of the baked semi-homo emerging spectrally from the upper-crust, to the *pate's* of Strasburg, the abnormally swollen livers of whose tormented geese roam the wide world to avenge upon gluttonous man the infamous tortures inflicted upon their original proprietors we must pass, too, the thousand-and-one ingenious inventions which adorn the pages of Messrs. Glass and Rumbold, by means of which dyspepsias arc produced *secundum artem*, and the valetudinarian is accustomed to retard his convalescence according to the most approved and fashionable mode.

The great pie of 1850, prepared by the ingenious Soyer, at the cost of a hundred guineas, for the especial delectation of municipal stomachs at York, is, likewise, altogether out of our way. Our business is with the pie that is sold for a penny, and sold in London. Let us add, moreover, that we treat only of the pie which is fairly worth a penny, leaving altogether out of our category the flimsy sophistries of your professed confectioner.

From time immemorial the wandering pieman was a prominent character in the highways and byways of London. He was generally a merry dog, and was always found where merriment was going on. Furnished with a tray about a yard square, either carried upon his head or suspended by a strap in front of his breast, he scrupled not to force his way through the thickest crowd, knowing that the very centre of action was the best market for his wares. He was a gambler, both from inclination and principle, and would toss with his customers, either by the dallying shilli-shally process of 'best five in nine,' the tricksy manoeuvre of 'best two in three,' or the desperate dash of 'sudden death!' in which latter case the first toss was destiny – a pie for a halfpenny, or your half-penny gone for nothing; but he invariably declined the mysterious

> *"the* ***wandering*** *pieman was a prominent* ***character*** *in the highways and byways of* ***London***"

process of 'the odd man;' not being altogether free from suspicion on the subject of collusion between a couple of hungry customers.

We meet with him frequently in old prints; and in Hogarth's 'March to Finchley,' there he stands in the very centre of the crowd, grinning with delight at the adroitness of one robbery, while he is himself the victim of another. We learn from this admirable figure by the greatest painter of English life, that the pieman of the last century perambulated the streets in professional costume; and we gather further, from the burly dimensions of his wares, that he kept his trade alive by the laudable practice of giving 'a good pennyworth for a penny.' Justice compels us to observe that his successors of a later generation have not been very conscientious observers of this maxim.

The varying price of flour, alternating with a sliding-scale, probably drove some of them to their wit's end; and perhaps this cause more than any other operated in imparting that complexion to their productions which made them resemble the dead body of a penny pie, and which in due time lost them favour with the discerning portion of their customers. Certain it is that the perambulating pie business in London fell very much into disrepute and contempt for several years before the abolition of the corn-laws and the advent of free trade. Opprobrious epithets were hurled at the wandering merchant as he paraded the streets and alleys — epithets which were in no small degree justified by the clammy and clay-like appearance of his goods. By degrees the profession got into disfavour, and the pieman either altogether disappeared, or merged in a dealer in foreign nuts, fruits, and other edibles which barred the suspicion of sophistication.

Still the relish for pies survived in the public taste, and the willing penny was as ready as ever to guerdon the man who, on fair grounds, would meet the general desire. No sooner, therefore, was the sliding-scale gone to the dogs, and a fair prospect of permanence offered to the speculator, in the guarantee of something like a fixed cost in the chief ingredient used, than up sprung almost simultaneously in every district of the metropolis a new description of pie-shops, which rushed at once into popularity and prosperity.

Capital had recognised the leading want of the age, and brought the appliances of wealth and energy to supply it. Avoiding, on the one hand, the glitter and pretension of the confectioner, and on the other the employment of adulterating or inferior materials, they produced an article which the populace devoured with universal commendation, to the gradual but certain profit of the projectors.

The peripatetic merchant was pretty generally driven out of the field by the superiority of the delicacy with which he had to compete. He could not manufacture on a small scale in a style to rival his new antagonists, and he could not purchase of them to sell again, because they would not allow him a living margin-boasting, as it would appear with perfect truth, that they sold at a small and infinitesimal profit, which would not bear division.

These penny-pie shops now form one of the characteristic features of the London trade in comestibles. That they are an immense convenience as well as a luxury to a very large section of the population, there can be no doubt. It might be imagined, at first view, that they would naturally seek a cheap locality and a low rental. This, however, is by no means the universal practice. In some of the chief lines of route they are to be found in full operation; and it is rare indeed, unless at seasons when the weather is very unfavourable, that they are not seen well filled with customers. They abound especially in the immediate neighbourhood of omnibus and cab stations, and very much in the thoroughfares and short – cuts most frequented by the middle and lower classes. But though the window may be of plate-glass, behind which piles of the finest fruit, joints, and quarters of the best meat, a large dish of silver eels, and a portly china bowl charged with a liberal heap of minced-meat, with here and there a few pies, lie temptingly arranged upon napkins of snowy whiteness, yet there is not a chair, stool, or seat of any kind to be found within. No dallying is looked for, nor would it probably be allowed. 'Pay for your pie, and go,' seems the order of the day. True, you may eat it there, as thousands do; but you must eat it standing, and clear of the counter.

We have more than once witnessed this interesting operation with mingled mirth and satisfaction; nay, what do we care? – take the confession for what it is worth – *pars ipsi fuimus* – we have eaten our pies (and paid for them too, no credit being given) – *in loco*, and are therefore in a condition to guarantee the truth of what we record. With few exceptions (we include ourselves among the number); there are no theoretical philosophers among the frequenters of the penny-pie shop.

The philosophy of bun-eating may be very profound, and may present, as we think it does, some difficult points; but the philosophy of penny-pie eating is absolutely next to *nil*. The customer of the pie-shop is a man (if he is not a boy) with whom a penny is a penny, and a pie is a pie, who, when he has the former to spend or the latter to eat, goes through the ceremony like one impressed with the settled conviction that he has business in hand which it behoves him to attend to. Look at him as he stands in the centre of the floor, erect as a grenadier, turning his busy mouth full upon the living tide that rushes along Holborn! Of shame or confusion of face in connection with the enviable position in which he stands he has not the remotest conception, and could as soon be brought to comprehend the *differential calculus* as to entertain a thought of it. What, we ask, would philosophy do for him? Still every customer is not so happily organised, and so blissfully insensible to the attacks of false shame; and for such as are unprepared for the public gaze, or constitutionally averse from it, a benevolent provision is made by a score of old play-bills stuck against the adverse wall, or swathing the sacks of flour which stand ready for use, and which they may peruse, or affect to peruse, in silence, munching their pennyworths the while.

"a good pennyworth for a penny"

The main body of the pie-eaters are, however, perfectly at their ease, and pass the very few minutes necessary for the discussion of their purchases in bandying compliments with three or four good-looking lasses, the very incarnations of good-temper and cleanly tidiness, who from morn to night are as busy as bees in extricating the pies from their metallic moulds, as they are demanded by the customers. These assistants lead no lazy life, but they are without exception plump and healthy-looking, and would seem (if we are to believe the report of an employer) to have an astonishing tendency to the parish church of the district in which they officiate, our informant having been bereaved of three by marriage in the short space of six months. Relays are necessary in most establishments on the main routes; as the shops are open all night long, seldom closing much before three in the morning when situated in the neighbourhood of a theatre or a cab-stand. Of the amount of business done in the course of a year it is not easy to form an estimate. Some pie-houses are known to consume as much flour as a neighbouring baker standing in the same track. The baker makes ninety quartern loaves from the sack of flour, and could hardly make a living upon less than a dozen sacks a week; but as the proportion borne by the crust of a penny-pie to a quartern loaf is a mystery which we have not yet succeeded in penetrating, we are wanting in the elements of an exact calculation.

"the delicate odour of mince-meat assails the passer-by, and reminds him that Christmas is coming"

The establishment of these shops has by degrees prodigiously increased the number of pie-eaters and the consumption of pies. Thousands and tens of thousands who would decline the handling of a scalding hot morsel in the public street, will yet steal to the corner of a shop, and in front of an old play-bill, delicately dandling the titbit on their fingertips till it cools to the precise temperature at which it is so delicious to swallow – 'snatch a fearful joy.' The tradesman, too, in the immediate vicinity, soon learns to appreciate the propinquity of the pie-shop, in the addition it furnishes to a cold dinner, and for half the sum it would have cost him if prepared in his own kitchen. Many a time and oft have we dropped in, upon the strength of a general invitation, at the dinner-table of an indulgent bibliopole, and recognised the undeniable pates of 'over the way' following upon the heels of the cold sirloin. With artisans out of work, and with town-travellers of small trade, the pie-shop is a halting-place, its productions presenting a cheap substitute for a dinner.

Few purchases are made before twelve o'clock in the day; in fact the shutters are rarely pulled down much before eleven; yet even then business is carried on for nearly twenty hours out of the twenty-four. About noon the current of custom sets in, and all hands are busy till four or five o'clock; after which there is a pause, or rather a relaxation, until evening, when the various bands of operatives, as they are successively released from work, again renew the tide. As these disappear, the numberless nightly exhibitions, lecture-rooms, mechanics' institutes, concerts, theatres and casinos, pour forth their motley hordes, of whom a large and hungry section find their way to the pie-house as the only available resource -the public-houses being shut up for the night, and the lobster-rooms, oyster saloons, 'shades,' 'coal-holes,' and 'cider-cellars,'' too expensive for the means of the multitude. After these come the cab-drivers, who, having conveyed to their homes the more moneyed classes of sight-seers and playgoers, return to their stands in the vicinity of the shop, and now consider that they may conscientiously indulge in a refreshment of eel-pies, winding up with a couple of 'fruiters,' to the amount at least of the sum of which they may have been able to cheat their fares.

Throughout the summer months the pie trade flourishes with unabated vigour. Each successive fruit, as it ripens and comes to market, adds a fresh impetus to the traffic. As autumn waxes, every week supplies a new attraction and a delicious variety; as it wanes into winter, good store of apples are laid up for future use; and so soon as Jack Frost sets his cold toes upon the pavement, the delicate odour of mince-meat assails the passer-by, and reminds him that Christmas is coming, and that the pieman is ready for him. It is only in the early spring that the pie-shop is under a temporary cloud. The apples of the past year are well nigh gone, and the few that remain have lost their succulence, and are dry and flavourless. This is the precise season when, as the pieman in 'Pickwick' too candidly observed, 'fruits is out, and cats is in.' Now there is an unaccountable prejudice against cats among the pie-devouring population of the metropolis; we are superior to it ourselves, and can therefore afford to mention it dispassionately, and to express our regret that any species of commerce, much more one so grateful to the palate, and so convenient to the purse, should periodically suffer declension through the prevalence of an unfounded prejudice.

Certain it is that penny-pie eating does materially decline about the early spring season; and it is certain too that, of late years, about the same season, a succession of fine Tabbies of our own have mysteriously disappeared. Attempts are made with rhubarb to combat the depression of business; but success in this matter is very partial – the generality of consumers being impressed with the popular notion that rhubarb is physic, and that physic is not fruit. But relief is at hand; the showers and sunshine of May bring the gooseberry to market; pies resume their importance; and the pieman, backed by an inexhaustible store of a fruit grateful to every English palate, commences the campaign with renewed energy, and bids defiance for the rest of the year to the mutations of fortune.

We shall close this sketch with a legend of the day, for the truth of which, however, we do not personally vouch. It was related and received with much gusto at an annual supper lately given by a large pie proprietor to his assembled hands – Some time since, so runs the current narrative, the owner of a thriving mutton-pie concern, which, after much difficulty, he had succeeded in establishing with borrowed capital, died before he had well extricated himself from the responsibilities of debt. The widow carried on the business after his decease, and throve so well, that a speculating baker on the opposite side of the way made her the offer of his hand. The lady refused, and the enraged suitor, determined on revenge, immediately converted his baking into an opposition pie-shop; and acting on the principle universal among London bakers, of doing business for the

"a succession of fine Tabbies of our own have mysteriously disappeared"

first month or two at a loss, made his pies twice as big as he could honestly afford to make them. The consequence was that the widow lost her custom, and was hastening fast to ruin, when a friend of her late husband, who was also a small creditor, paid her a visit. She detailed her grievance to him, and lamented her lost trade and fearful prospects. 'Ho, ho!' said her friend, 'that ere's the move, is it? Never you mind, my dear. If I don't git your trade agin, there aint no snakes, mark me – that's all!' So saying he took his leave.

About eight o'clock the same evening, when the baker's new pie-shop was crammed to overflowing, and the principal was below superintending the production of a new batch, in walks the widow's friend in the costume of a kennel-raker, and elbowing his way to the counter, dabs down upon it a brace of huge dead cats, vociferating at the same time to the astonished damsel in attendance; 'Tell your master, my dear, as how them two makes six-and-thirty this week, and say I'll bring t'other four to-morrer arternoon!' With that he swaggered out and went his way. So powerful was the prejudice against cat-mutton among the population of that neighbourhood that the shop was clear in an instant, and the floor was seen covered with hastily-abandoned specimens of every variety of segments of a circle? The spirit-shop at the corner of the street experienced an unusually large demand for 'goes' of brandy, and interjectional ejaculations not purely grammatical were not merely audible, but visible too in the district. It is averred that the ingenious expedient of the widow's friend, founded as it was upon a profound knowledge of human prejudices, had the desired effect of restoring 'the balance of trade.' The widow recovered her commerce; the resentful baker was clone as brown as if he had been shut up in his own oven; and the friend who brought about this measure of justice received the hand of the lady as a reward for his interference.

From *Curiosities of London Life; or,
Phases Physiological and Social of the Great Metropolis*
by Charles Manby Smith, 1853

Pastry

There is an old cooks' saying that people with cold hands are good at making pastry, and it is true that shortcrust, puff and all their relatives do need to be kept cool for best results. But really everyone can succeed in making excellent pastry with the right ingredients, some useful tips and just a little practice. So don't be afraid to have a go at making your own; it's better, cheaper and purer than the bought stuff, and you can't beat the satisfaction of knowing that you've created the whole pie, not just done an assembly job!

Always keep the off-cuts of raw pastry and use them to patch any small cracks or holes that may develop during baking that would allow the sauce to leak out.

FLOURS

Regular white plain flour is the best choice for most pastries, giving a light texture and crisp finish. The high gluten content of strong or bread flour makes the pastry too elastic, so should be avoided. Italian type '0' and '00' flours, which are soft and finely milled, are also good for making pastry. People with allergies to wheat and gluten need not forgo pies and tarts, though, thanks to the ready availability of gluten-free flours. While they are not suitable for pastries such as puff and flaky, they can simply be substituted for the wheat flour in shortcrust recipes.

Pastry made with wholemeal flour usually requires a little extra water, and some recipes will include baking powder or bicarbonate of soda to help lighten the texture.

Remember, pastry is only as good as the flours you use, so don't buy cheap ones!

FATS

Using equal quantities of butter and lard is a good idea for shortcrust and flaky pastries. Butter gives pastry an excellent flavour and crisp texture, while lard, though it doesn't add flavour, makes pastry short and flaky.

Margarine can be used to make pastry but it will not taste as good as that made with butter. Vegetable shortening (a solid fat made from hydrogenated vegetable oils) lightens the texture and is a vegetarian alternative to lard.

Some recipes incorporate oil, usually in an effort to replace the saturated fats of butter or lard with healthier polyunsaturates and monounsaturates. However, oil can make the dough difficult to handle and its use also compromises the flavour and texture of the cooked pastry. The greasy finish means it is best suited to savoury recipes.

Pastries made with cream cheese or sour cream in place of some of the fat will tend not to be flaky but will have rich dairy taste.

Suet is a rich form of solid white fat that is usually derived from the fat surrounding beef kidneys. It is sold ready-grated and dusted with flour. Vegetarian alternatives are readily available, although people who wish to avoid the hydrogenated vegetable oils from which these are made may like to try finely ground brazil nuts as a substitute.

MAKING PASTRY

It is best to chill the ingredients and utensils before making pastry, and to use a cool working surface – marble is ideal. Traditionally, pastry was made first thing in the morning, before the kitchen had a chance to get hot in the heat of the sun or the ovens. With refrigeration, of course, you can decide to prepare pastry at any time of the day – or night!

Pastry needs to be mixed quickly to help keep it cool and also minimise development of the flour's gluten content, otherwise the pastry may become too elastic, difficult to roll, inclined to shrink, and tough in texture. Too much handling can also make the fat soft and the finished pastry greasy.

When making shortcrust, a food processor can be an advantage in that it can help minimise handling. However, it is important not to let the machine overwork the pastry – take it out as soon as it forms a lump.

Once the dough is formed, chilling it for 30 minutes or so helps relax the gluten and set the fat, making the dough manageable and less likely to shrink. Chilling the dough between each stage of making puff pastry is vital. Raw shortcrust, puff and flaky pastries can be kept wrapped in cling film in the fridge for two or three days before rolling and baking, and can also be frozen for up to three months.

ROLLING

You need a large, cool working surface when rolling pastry, and one that is well dusted with flour to prevent sticking. You can roll the pastry out on a special pastry cloth that shows the dimensions required for various tart tins, or between layers of cling film or greaseproof paper, but this isn't essential. Ensure you have a long, strong rolling pin, the standard one being 18 inches (around 45 cm).

Liberally dust the rolling pin and pastry lightly with flour to prevent it from sticking and roll gently and evenly, turning the pastry occasionally to keep it from sticking and to help to give you an even circle, square, etc. Try to flatten and smooth the pastry rather than pull or stretch it, as the latter will just lead to tearing and shrinkage.

Always use a flat surface or a pastry board that is lightly floured. Shape the pastry first either into a round or oblong and then roll with both hands, keeping the pressure even. Give the pastry a quarter turn and roll away from you, repeating this process until the pastry is the size you require. I always roll larger than required and use the excess pastry to make leaves or other shapes to decorate my pies. With most pastries you will be aiming for a thickness of $1/5$th of an inch (0.3 cm).

LINING TINS, TRAYS AND BOWLS

The standard size of dish for a family of four is a 23 cm × 2 cm / 9 inch × ¾ inch deep pie dish. To line a dish of this size the pastry would have to be rolled out to a 30 cm / 12-inch diameter, to leave excess dough to hang over the edge of the pie dish. For the top of the pie it would have to be rolled out to 25.5 cm / 10 inches in diameter.

When lining a tart tin, it's a good idea to curl your rolled pastry over the rolling pin and use that to help you transfer the pastry to the tin. Gently ease the pastry into the corners of the tin, press well into position and allow it to rest again before trimming off the excess pastry. While the oven is pre-heating, rest the lined tin in the fridge to prevent shrinkage during cooking.

A LESSON IN BAKING BLIND

How many times has your pie or tart fallen apart because of a soggy pie case? Too many I imagine! The simple way to avoid this common problem, however, is blind baking, where you fully pre-bake the pastry in the tin before adding the filling and cooking the whole pie again, with its lid if it has one. Blind baking ensures that the pastry is crisp, leak proof and does not rise and have bubbles in it. Flaky and puff pastries and straight-sided pies are not usually blind baked, but with pies made with other pastries you may decide to blind bake, particularly where the contents are more liquid.

To 'bake blind' you simply place the pastry-lined tin on a baking tray (this makes it easier to remove from the oven when hot) and tear off a sheet of baking parchment or greaseproof paper. Lay it in the pastry case so that it comes up the sides a little and tip in some ceramic baking beans, dried peas or uncooked rice. The idea is to weight the paper and pastry down to prevent it from rising up during baking.

It also helps to prevent sauces from making your pastry base soggy if you place the tart tin on a pre-heated baking sheet while cooking, and part way through you can glaze the pastry with beaten egg to make a really good seal. Some cooks like to prick the bottom of the pastry with a fork before baking blind, but I find this unnecessary. Besides, any holes in your pastry can allow a liquid filling to seep out before it sets.

Most pastries should blind cook at a fairly high temperature, usually 190–200°C / 375–400°F / gas mark 5–6. Make sure the oven is up to the correct temperature before baking the pastry or it tends to 'melt' and slide down the sides of the dish before setting. After around 9–12 minutes, when the case is a lovely sandy colour, remove it from the oven and gently lift off the paper and baking beans. Place back in the oven for another 2–3 minutes to finish. A good way to tell if a shortcrust pastry case is done is to rub it gently with your third finger then rub against your thumb. It should feel slightly gritty, like fine sand, and is now ready for filling.

Shortcrust pastry

350 g / 12 oz plain flour

Pinch of salt

50 g / 2 oz lard

100 g / 4 oz butter

80 ml / 5 tablespoons cold
   water, approx

MAKES 1 lb

Sift the flour with the salt. Rub in the lard and butter until it looks like breadcrumbs.

Add just enough water to the mixture to form a firm dough.

Chill for 20 minutes and then let it relax for 10 minutes after rolling out.

Rich shortcrust pastry

350 g / 12 oz plain flour

Pinch of salt

200 g / 8 oz butter

1 egg yolk

80 ml / 5 tablespoons cold
   water, approx

MAKES 1 lb

Sift the flour with the salt. Rub in the butter until it looks like breadcrumbs. Mix the egg yolk with half the water and then add to the mixture.

Add just enough of the remaining water to the mixture to form a firm dough.

Chill for 20 minutes and then let it relax for 10 minutes after rolling out.

Wholemeal shortcrust

100 g / 4 oz wholemeal flour

100 g / 4 oz self-raising flour

Pinch of salt

50 g / 2 oz butter

50 g / 2 oz lard

40 ml / 2½ tablespoons cold
    water, approx

MAKES 12 oz

Mix the flours with the salt. Rub in the butter and lard until it looks like breadcrumbs.

Add just enough water to the mixture to form a firm dough.

Chill for 20 minutes and then let it relax for 10 minutes after rolling out.

Only use salt and black pepper in a savoury crust: if using beef add a teaspoon of thyme; use rosemary or mint for lamb; and sage for chicken

Savoury pasty pastry

350 g / 12 oz plain flour

175 g / 6 oz lard

Salt and black pepper

100 ml / 6 tablespoons cold
    water, approx

MAKES 1 lb

Sift the flour. Rub in the lard adding the salt and pepper and mix thoroughly until it looks like breadcrumbs.

Add just enough water to the mixture to form a firm dough.

Place the pastry into a plastic bag and put into the fridge for 20 minutes.

My mum & gran's suet crust pastry

350 g / 12 oz self-raising flour

175 g / 6 oz shredded beef suet

100 ml / 6 tablespoons cold
water, approx

Salt and black pepper

MAKES 1 lb

Sift the flour, salt and pepper into a bowl, then add the suet and mix in lightly with your hands or a fork. Add some cold water, mixing in with a bladed knife for the first minute, and then use your fingers, mixing until the bowl is clean.

Let the suet pastry rest for 10 minutes before using it.

This can also be used as a **game pastry** for oven baking rather than steaming.

Traditional suet crust (from 1890)

225 g / 8 oz self-raising flour

1 level teaspoon baking powder

100 g / 4 oz shredded beef suet

Salt and white pepper

Pinch of mace

Pinch of ground rosemary

60 ml / 4 tablespoons cold
water, approx

MAKES 12 oz

Sift the flour, salt, pepper and spices, then add the suet and mix in lightly with your hands or a fork.

Make a well in the centre of the mixture and add just enough water to make workable dough.

Knead for a few minutes only and then the suet pastry is ready for immediate use.

This crust was always used for game pies

Game suet pastry

350 g / 12 oz plain flour

100 g / 4 oz shredded suet

Salt and black pepper

150 g / 6 oz softened unsalted
  butter

1 egg yolk

120 ml / 8 tablespoons cold
  water

MAKES 1 lb

Sift the flour into a mixing bowl, add the suet, salt and pepper.

Rub in the butter lightly with your fingertips, and when the mixture resembles fine breadcrumbs. Mix the egg yolk with half the water and then add to the mixture.

Add just enough of the remaining water to the mixture to form a firm dough.

Knead the dough lightly for 4 minutes, then cover and leave in a warm place until required.

Hot water pastry

150 g / 5 oz lard

200 ml / 7 fl oz hot water

350 g / 12 oz plain flour with
  ½ teaspoon salt

1 large egg yolk

1.4 litre / 2½ pint round loaf
  dish or baking dish, greased
  and lined with greaseproof
  paper, or 6 small pie tins,
  greased and lined with
  greaseproof paper

MAKES 1 lb

Put the lard and water into a saucepan and heat gently until the lard has melted. Bring to the boil, remove from the heat and beat in the seasoned flour to form soft dough.

Beat the egg yolk into the dough, cover the dough with a damp cloth and rest it in a warm place for 15 minutes. Do not allow the dough to cool.

Roll out the pastry and pat two-thirds of it into the base and around the pie dish evenly distributed to make the shape. Reserve the rest of the hot water pastry for the top.

Rough puff pastry

450 g / 1 lb strong plain flour

Pinch of salt

350 ml / 12 fl oz cold water, approx

Juice of half a lemon

450 g / 1 lb unsalted butter

MAKES 2 lb

Sift the flour and salt into a bowl and mix to a firm dough with the water and lemon juice.

Place the dough into greaseproof paper and rest in the fridge for 25 minutes.

Roll the dough into a square about 1 cm / ½ inch thick.

Cut the butter into 2 cm / 1 inch dice and scatter into the centre of the dough. Fold the dough over the pieces of butter to make a parcel shape.

Flour the working area and roll out the dough into a rectangle, approximately 45 cm × 15 cm (18 ins × 6 ins). Fold the dough into 3 with the sides aligned, sealing the edges.

Turn the dough through 90 degrees. Repeat the rolling and folding process again sealing the edges. Cover with cling film and chill for a further 15 minutes.

Repeat the rolling a third time, liberally flouring the working area and rolling pin, until you have another 45 cm × 15 cm rectangle. Fold the dough into 3 again, with the sides aligned, sealing the edges.

Turn the dough through 90 degrees. Repeat the rolling and folding process one more time, again sealing the edges.

Cover with cling film and chill for a further 30 minutes and the puff pastry is now ready for use.

Traditional puff pastry

225 g / 8 oz plain flour

Pinch of salt

30 g / 1 oz lard

150 ml / ¼ pint ice-cold water

2 tablespoons lemon juice

200 g / 7 oz butter

MAKES 1 lb

Sift the flour and the salt. Gently rub in the lard with your fingers. Add the ice water and lemon juice and mix with a knife to a dough consistency. Turn the dough onto the table or worktop and knead very quickly until it is smooth. Wrap in cling film and leave in the fridge for 30 minutes.

Roll the dough into a square about 1 cm / ½ inch thick.

Cut the butter into 2 cm / 1 inch dice and scatter into the centre of the dough. Fold the dough over the pieces of butter to make a parcel shape.

Flour the working area and roll out the dough into a rectangle, approximately 45 cm × 15 cm (18 ins × 6 ins). Fold the dough into 3 with the sides aligned, sealing the edges.

Turn the dough through 90 degrees. Repeat the rolling and folding process again sealing the edges. Cover with cling film and chill for a further 30 minutes.

Repeat the rolling a third time, liberally flouring the working area and rolling pin, until you have another 45 cm × 15 cm rectangle. Fold the dough into 3 again, with the sides aligned, sealing the edges.

Turn the dough through 90 degrees. Repeat the rolling and folding process one more time, again sealing the edges.

Cover with cling film and chill for a further 30 minutes and the puff pastry is now ready for use.

Flaky pastry

170 g / 8 oz butter or a mixture
of butter and lard

225 g / 8 oz plain flour

120 ml / 8 tablespoons cold
water and 1 squeeze of
lemon juice

Pinch of salt

1 egg, beaten, to glaze

MAKES 1 lb

Flaky pastry can be used instead of puff pastry where a great rise is not needed; savoury pies, turnovers and sausage rolls all use it to great effect. Note: more water may be required to make the dough soft

Divide the butter into 4 equal portions. Chill 3 portions.

Sift flour and salt into a bowl. Rub in the unchilled portion of butter. Mix to a soft dough with the water and lemon juice. Turn out onto a floured work surface and knead thoroughly. Put into a polythene bag or wrap in aluminium foil. Chill for 30 minutes.

Roll out into a 0.5 cm / ¼ inch thick rectangle measuring about 45 cm × 15 cm (18 ins × 6 ins). Using the tip of a knife, dot the second portion of butter (in small flakes) over the top and middle thirds of the rectangle to within 2.5 cm / 1 inch of the edges. Dust lightly with flour.

Fold in 3 by bringing the bottom third over the middle third and folding the top third over. Seal the open edges by pressing firmly together with a rolling pin. Put into a polythene bag or wrap in aluminium foil. Chill for 15 minutes.

Remove from the bag or unwrap. With folded edges to left and right, roll out again into a 45 cm × 15 cm (18 ins × 6 ins) rectangle. Cover with a third of the butter as before. Fold, seal and chill. Repeat again, adding last portion of butter and chill.

Roll out again. Fold and seal, return to the polythene bag or aluminium foil. Chill for at least 30 minutes before rolling out to 0.5 cm / ¼ inch thickness and lining your tin etc. After shaping the pastry in the tin etc., let it rest for 30 minutes before baking.

For the lid, roll out the pastry on a lightly floured working surface to 0.3 cm / ⅛ inch thick and use as required. Brush with beaten egg before baking to give the characteristic glaze.

Bake at 200ºC / 400ºF / gas mark 6, unless otherwise stated.

Quick flaky pastry

225 g / 8 oz plain flour

175 g / 6 oz butter

60 ml / 4 tablespoons cold
water, approx

MAKES 1 lb

Sift the flour into a bowl, then rub in the butter and mix
thoroughly until it looks like breadcrumbs.

Add just enough water to the mixture to form a firm dough.

Place the pastry into a plastic bag and chill for 30 minutes.

Cheddar cheese pastry

350 g / 12 oz plain flour

175 g / 6 oz butter

100 g / 4 oz grated Cheddar
cheese

Pinch of salt, black pepper and
English mustard powder

1 egg yolk

60 ml / 4 tablespoons cold
water, approx

MAKES 1 lb

Sift the flour with the salt. Rub in the butter until it looks like
breadcrumbs. Mix the yolk with the water, grated cheese, pepper
and mustard and add to the mixture.

Mix to form a firm dough.

Chill for 20 minutes and then let it relax for 10 minutes after
rolling out.

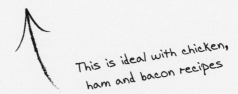

This is ideal with chicken,
ham and bacon recipes

Cobbler pastry

225 g / 8 oz self-raising flour

50 g / 2 oz vegetarian suet

2 tablespoons chopped fresh
  parsley and chives

40 g / 1½ oz butter

60 ml / 4 tablespoons plain
  yogurt

Water

Pinch of salt and black pepper

MAKES 1 lb

Sift the flour and stir in the suet, herbs and seasoning.

Rub in the butter with your fingertips until the mixture
resembles fine breadcrumbs.

Add the yogurt and enough cold water to make a soft dough.

The dough is now ready for any cobbler recipe.

Not-so-coarse wholemeal pastry

125 g / 5 oz wholemeal flour

125 g / 5 oz plain flour

½ teaspoon salt

50 g / 2 oz lard

50 g / 2 oz butter

60 ml / 4 tablespoons water

25 g / 1 oz cornflour

MAKES 1 lb

Mix the salt into the flour with your fingertips.

Rub in the fats until the mixture resembles breadcrumbs.

Add just enough of the water bind to bind the mixture
completely.

Gather into a ball with your fingertips and roll out on a board
lightly dredged with cornflour.

Calzone dough/pastry

25 g / 1 oz fresh yeast or
    ½ teaspoon or 1 pack active
    dry yeast
250 ml / 8 fl oz of warm
    (105–115 ºF / 42–45 ºC)
    water
Pinch of sugar
400 g / 14 oz plain flour
1 teaspoon of salt
2 tablespoons olive oil

MAKES 1 lb

Dissolve the yeast in the water, in a large mixing bowl and let it stand for 5 minutes. Add the remaining ingredients and mix, either by hand or with a mixer set to low speed, until the ingredients are blended.

Now hand-knead the dough, or mix it with a dough hook, on a low speed, for about 10 minutes, or until the dough is smooth and elastic. Coat the insides of another bowl with a little more olive oil and turn the dough into it to coat it with the oil, then cover with plastic wrap and set it in a warm place to rise for an hour, or until it doubles in volume, when it will be ready for use.

Pie stocks & sauces

The following stocks and methods are taken from my *200 Classic Sauces* cookbook – a bit of recipe recycling that shows that I really do waste nothing! In fact no good chef or cook will even throw away the water in which meat, fish or vegetables have been boiled, for these liquors, together with bones, giblets etc., are the foundations of a hearty stock. A good tip for the storage of stocks is to put them in kilner jars, or you can re-use glass pasta sauce etc. jars which have a 'clicky' sealable lid. Sterilise the jars then pour in the still-hot stock. Close the lids of kilner jars using the lid mechanism, or put the safety lid tightly onto recycled jars. As the liquid cools it will create a vacuum and suck in the lids, creating airtight seals (the 'clicky' part of the re-used jar lids will not click if the seal is good).

Basic poultry giblet stock

50 g / 2 oz duck fat

450 g / 1 lb mixed giblets from chicken and turkey

2 leeks

1 large onion

1 stick of celery

2 large carrots

2 sachet bouquet garni

4 white peppercorns

8 juniper berries

60 ml / 4 tablespoons white wine vinegar

1 litre / 1¾ pints chicken stock

1 sprig of thyme

Salt and black pepper

Heat the duck fat in a large saucepan, chop the giblets and add them to the duck fat along with the cleaned and sliced leeks, onion, celery and carrots. Cook for 10 minutes.

Add the rest of the ingredients and bring slowly to the boil, removing any scum from the surface and covering the saucepan with a tight-fitting lid.

Simmer the stock over a low heat for 90 minutes to extract all the flavour from the giblets and vegetables, topping up with hot water if the stock level falls below the ingredients.

Strain the stock through a fine sieve, into a large bowl. Leave to settle for 5 minutes, then remove the fat from the surface by drawing absorbent kitchen paper towel over it.

Adjust the seasoning and it is ready for use for a giblet soup or gravy.

Basic meat (brown) stock

900 g / 2 lb beef bones

450 g / 1 lb shin of Scottish beef

50 g / 2 oz dripping

2 leeks

1 large onion

1 stick of celery

2 large carrots

2 sachet bouquet garni

4 white peppercorns

60 ml / 4 tablespoons white
    wine vinegar

1 sprig of thyme

Salt and black pepper

Blanch the bones for 10 minutes in boiling water, and then put them, with the chopped meat and dripping, into a large roasting tin. Cook in the centre of the oven for 40 minutes at 220°C / 425°F / gas mark 7.

Put the bones into a large, deep casserole or pan, then add the cleaned and sliced vegetables and all the other ingredients. Cover with water and bring the contents slowly to the boil. Remove any scum from the surface and cover the casserole or pan with a tight-fitting lid.

Simmer the stock over the lowest heat for 3 hours to extract all the flavour from the bones and vegetables, topping up with hot water if the stock level falls below the ingredients.

Strain the stock through a fine sieve, into a large bowl. Leave the meat stock to settle for 5 minutes, and then remove the fat from the surface by drawing absorbent kitchen towel paper over it. Adjust the seasoning and it is ready for use.

NOTE: If making chicken stock then use the equivalent in weight of a full chicken, jointed and with the bones left in. To make a cow heel stock simply add the cow heel to the stock, save the meat from the shin and cow heel, and this will make a wonderful steak and cow heel pie.

Pork stock

Pork bones
1 pig's foot
1 litre / 1¾ pint water
1 large onion, peeled
1 carrot
1 bay leaf
2 sage leaves
1 sprig of thyme
1 sprig of marjoram
Salt
6 peppercorns

Make the stock by putting all the ingredients into a large pan, bringing to the boil and simmering for 3 hours or more until the stock has reduced to 300 ml / ½ pint.

Let it cool and skim off all the fat. Check the seasoning and when it is cold pour through a fine non-metallic sieve.

This stock will give you perfect pork pie jelly

Mutton & lamb stock

Lamb and mutton bones

1 shin of lamb

1 litre / 1¾ pint water

1 large onion, peeled

1 carrot

1 bay leaf

2 sage leaves

1 sprig of thyme

1 sprig of marjoram

Salt

6 peppercorns

Make the stock by putting all the ingredients into a large pan bringing to the boil and simmering for 3 hours or more until the stock has reduced to 300 ml / ½ pint.

Let it cool and skim off any fat. Check the seasoning and allow the stock to cool. Pour the stock through a fine non-metallic sieve and it is ready for use.

Chicken stock

Put raw chicken trimmings, giblets, feet, carcass (but NOT the skin) into a pan and add an onion, a celery stalk, a carrot, a leek and a bay leaf, along with 60 ml / 4 tablespoons white wine vinegar. Add 1.75 litres / 3 pints of water, season and simmer for 3 hours, skimming every 5 minutes. Pour through a fine sieve.

Freeze any leftover stock in ice cube trays

Game stock

900 g / 2 lb game bird carcass and bones

450 g / 1 lb shin of venison

1 pig's foot

50 g / 2 oz dripping

2 leeks

1 large onion

1 stick of celery

2 large carrots

2 sachet bouquets garni

4 tablespoons port

6 juniper berries

4 white peppercorns

60 ml / 4 tablespoons white wine vinegar

1 sprig of thyme

Salt and black pepper

Place the carcass, bones, venison and pig's foot into hot dripping in a large roasting tin. Brown in the centre of the oven for 20 minutes at 220°C / 425°F / gas mark 7.

Put the bones in a large, deep casserole or pan; add the cleaned and sliced vegetables and all the other ingredients. Cover with 1 litre / 1¾ pints water and bring the contents slowly to the boil. Remove any scum from the surface and cover the casserole or pan with a tight-fitting lid.

Simmer over the lowest heat for 3 hours to extract all the flavour from the bones and vegetables, topping up with hot water if the level of stock should fall below the ingredients.

Strain the stock through a fine sieve, into a large bowl. Leave the meat stock to settle for 5 minutes, and then remove the fat from the surface by drawing absorbent kitchen paper towel over it.

Adjust the seasoning and the game stock is ready for use.

VARIATION: You can make a game stock using venison, guinea fowl, quail, hare and rabbit bones. Using the brown veal stock with the addition of 6 juniper berries and 60 ml / 4 tablespoons red wine vinegar, thyme and a little sprig of rosemary.

Vegetable stock

1 carrot

1 leek

1 onion

1 swede

4 shallots

1 parsnip

1 stick of celery

1 turnip

60 ml / 4 tablespoons white wine vinegar

For vegetable stock it is very important that you use large pieces of fresh, clean vegetables, except cabbage, cauliflower and sprouts, as they have an overpowering taste and smell and will dominate the stock.

Use carrots, leeks, onions, swede, shallots, parsnip, celery and turnip. Cover with water, add 60 ml / 4 tablespoons white wine vinegar and simmer for 1 hour, seasoning well.

Pour through a fine sieve, cool and store in the fridge until the stock is required.

Fish stock

- 1.8 kg / 4 lb fish bones
- 50 g / 2 oz butter
- 200 g / 8 oz onion, finely chopped
- 200 g / 8 oz leek, finely chopped
- 200 g / 8 oz celery, finely chopped
- Juice of 1 lemon
- 8 peppercorns
- 1 bay leaf
- Sprig of parsley
- 150 ml / 5 fl oz of white wine
- 2 litres / 3½ pints water
- 60 ml / 4 tablespoons white wine vinegar

Thoroughly wash the fish bones and roughly chop them up. Melt the butter in a large pan and put in the chopped vegetables, frying for 3 minutes until they are slightly soft.

Add the fish bones and the remainder of the ingredients except the water. Cook for 8 minutes until the liquid is slightly reduced, then add the water, bring to the boil, skim and simmer for 30 minutes.

Where possible include in your fish bones the heads, skins and trimmings, and you can also use cheap white fish. Make use of the bones from monkfish, turbot, whiting and sole, but don't use oily fish such as mackerel or herrings.

Pass the stock through a sieve and allow it to cool. After 1 hour it is then ready for use.

Fish stock can be frozen, or use it fresh within 48 hours

Basic white (béchamel) sauce

A béchamel or white sauce is the starting point for all milk-based sauces. From this base you can add a wide range of ingredients to suit the recipe or your personal preferences. For example, just add one finely chopped, gently sautéd onion to make an onion sauce; 2 tablespoons of very finely chopped parsley for parsley sauce; or you could try my special cheese sauce recipe below. Most of the recipes in this book have their own sauces – built into them, as it were – but you might like to add your own saucy gravy to the finished dish. Go forth and experiment!

300 ml / ½ pint of fresh milk

½ white onion, cut into quarters

½ carrot, peeled and sliced

1 bay leaf

1 blade of mace

1 sprig of parsley

3 black peppercorns

Pinch of nutmeg and thyme

15 g/ ½ oz butter

15 g/ ½ oz flour

Salt and white pepper

50 ml/ 3 tablespoons double cream

Gently heat the milk in the saucepan and add the onion, carrot, peppercorns, mace, nutmeg, thyme and parsley. Cover the pan with a lid and gently simmer without boiling for 10 minutes. Remove the pan from the heat and leave the milk to infuse for a further 12 minutes and then strain and place to one side.

Melt the butter in a pan, stir in the flour. Cook over a low heat, stirring occasionally, and when it becomes light in colour and crumbly in texture (about 12 minutes) take the pan off the heat and allow the mixture to cool.

Add the strained milk slowly to make a very smooth sauce, cooking gently for 4 minutes. Season with the salt and pepper, then slowly blend in the cream for a light, smooth texture.

Basic cheese sauce

1 egg yolk

15 ml / 1 tablespoon double cream

300 ml / ½ pint béchamel sauce

50 g / 2 oz grated Parmesan

Mix the egg yolks with the cream and add a little warmed béchamel. Blend the mixture with the remaining béchamel, then add the grated cheese and combine thoroughly, warming up again if needed.

Instead of Parmesan try using your favourite cheese, such as Cheddar, Stilton or Lancashire

Bring on the pies

Pork & ham

Perhaps the most famous and quintessentially British of all pies is the pork pie. A good one, with a lovely, crunchy, raised pastry case housing a tasty filling surrounded with succulent jelly, really can't be beaten. Arguably the best of all is the Melton Mowbray, with its characteristically bowed (rather than straight) sides formed from melt-in-the-mouth, dark caramel-coloured pastry. But pork (and ham) is a wonderfully versatile ingredient, and there is an almost endless variety of tastes and combinations that can be achieved using it. So let the Melton Mowbray inspire you to use the recipes in this chapter to have a go at other types of pork pie that you will really enjoy at home.

A Real Lancashire Pork Pie

This is a classic recipe from eighteenth-century Lancashire which should be served with English mustard and a Cox's Orange Pippin apple salad. I must admit to being biased and I reckon that the best pork pies in Lancashire are made at Waterfields bakery in Leigh, near Wigan. They use the finest local pork, which is essential for the flavour of their pie.

I made my Lancashire pork pies, using the recipe below, for wine expert and fellow pie-lover Jilly Goolden at the 2010 Wigan Food and Drink Festival. She took them home and I was really touched when she wrote to me the next day, in her inimitable style, to say that 'it was great to see you again and much fun working with you – and tasting all the delicacies you had so brilliantly prepared. But none so brilliantly as the pork pies you charmingly sent me away with; they were gorgeously delicious – a real triumph. Thank you, thank you!'

For a real twist on this pie boil 12 quails eggs for 4 minutes, plunge them into ice-cold water for 4 minutes and carefully peel away the soft shells. When you are making the pies, carefully place 2 quails eggs into the centre of the pork mix in each and you will then have mini gala pies, which will be a nice surprise for your guests when they bite into them!

Hot water pastry

150 g / 5 oz lard

200 ml / 7 fl oz hot water

350 g / 12 oz plain flour
   seasoned with
   ½ teaspoon salt

1 large egg yolk

Pie filling

700 g / 1½ lb of pork shoulder,
   ⅓ fat, diced very small into
   5 mm / ¼ inch cubes, skin
   and gristle removed

Generous pinch of salt

Generous pinch of white pepper

1 teaspoon anchovy essence

1 egg, beaten, to glaze

Pork stock
   (see recipe on page 48)

SERVES 4

Combine all the pie filling ingredients into a large bowl, with 3 tablespoons of the pork stock.

Let the pork mixture rest, meanwhile make up the hot water pastry as shown on page 36 and roll out. Pat two-thirds of the pastry into a lightly greased pie mould or cake tin about 18 cm / 7 inches in diameter with hinged sides and a detachable base. Evenly distribute the pastry to make the pie shape, reserving the remaining third for the top.

Carefully place the pie case onto a baking tray and put in the seasoned pork filling. Top with the pastry lid, firmly crimping the edges, being very careful not to break the case. Make a hole in the centre of the lid to allow the steam out during the cooking process. Bake in the lower part of the oven for 2 hours at 150°C / 300°F / gas mark 2.

10 minutes before the end of cooking time, egg-glaze the pie and return to the oven.

Once cooking is completed, turn the oven off without opening the door and leave the pie in to dry naturally for 1 hour.

Reheat the stock until just warm and pour into the hole in the top of the pie, as much stock as the pie will hold.

Let the pie cool, wrap in cling film and refrigerate for at least 1 day. Take one slice from the pie and hide it for yourself before all your hard work is devoured!

In Lancashire when I was growing up they used to say that with pigs 'everything is used except the squeak', meaning there really is very little waste, something that is very close to my heart

Chester Pork Pye

The first recorded recipe for a pork pie was in 1390 in the kitchen of the court of King Richard II. Most pork pies in Britain contain only pork and are modelled on the famous pork pies of Melton Mowbray, the first town to produce pork pies commercially in England. What many people don't know, however, is that there is an older version of the pork pie that originates from much further north: the Cheshire Pork Pye consists of layers of pork and apple, sweetened with sugar, and I've included the recipe for it (see page 62) from the *Art of Cookery made plain and easy* by Mrs Hannah Glasse, written in 1747, together with my own revised version, Chester Pork Pye.

450 g / 1 lb shortcrust pastry (see recipe on page 33)

650 g / 1 lb 6 oz lean, minced pork

4 rashers of naturally cured bacon, diced

Salt and black pepper

Nutmeg, grated

1 teaspoon dried sage

4 Cox's Orange Pippin apples, cored and sliced

75 g / 3 oz sugar

200 ml / 7 fl oz dry white wine

200 g / 7 oz butter

1 egg, beaten, to glaze

SERVES 4

Roll out the pastry and line a 18 cm / 7 inch pie dish, remembering to roll out enough pastry to make the lid too.

Mix together the pork and bacon in a bowl and season with the salt, pepper, nutmeg and sage.

Arrange a layer of pork in the bottom of the dish, then a layer of apple tossed in sugar and continue with alternate layers until the dish is full.

Pour in the white wine and dot the top of the mixture with butter.

Put the pie lid on top and make a slit in the pastry. Glaze with a little egg.

Bake in the oven at 220°C / 425°F / gas mark 7 for 15 minutes, then reduce the heat to 190°C / 375°F / gas mark 5 and bake for a further 45 minutes.

Serve hot or cold. Traditionally it was served hot with peas, now it is more usually eaten cold.

Nineteenth-century Cheshire Pork Pie

This variation still has the combination of savoury and sweet but in different proportions and with a puff pastry – rather than shortcrust – case.

1 kg / 2¼ lb pork loin or loin steaks, diced

3 Cox's eating apples, cored and sliced

1 small onion, peeled and chopped

Salt and black pepper

Nutmeg, grated

1 teaspoon sugar

275 ml / 10 fl oz white wine, or a combination of white wine and vegetable stock

500 g / 1 lb 2 oz puff pastry (see recipe on page 39)

1 egg, beaten, to glaze

SERVES 4–6

Pre-heat the oven to 180°C / 350°F / gas mark 4.

In a deep pie dish, layer the pork, apples and onion, seasoning well with salt, pepper, nutmeg and sugar as you go. Pour over the wine or wine and stock.

Roll out the pastry slightly larger than the pie dish. Brush the dish rim with beaten egg, stick on the pastry trim to form a border, and then brush this with beaten egg.

Top with the pastry lid, press the edges together firmly to seal, then make slits, steam holes, or even an open space in the top and brush the lid well with beaten egg.

Bake in the oven for about 1 hour to ensure that the meat is cooked – you may have to lay a piece of baking paper on top after about 30 minutes to prevent the pastry from browning too much.

The Cheshire Pork Pie

This pie is similar to a Fitchett pie which used to be made with mutton and was called a Dartmouth pie in the West Country. In Cheshire they use fresh pork instead of bacon or mutton.

Take a Loin of pork, skin it, cut it into steaks.
Season it with salt, nutmeg and pepper.

Make a good crust, lay a layer of pork then a layer of pippins pared and cored, a little sugar, enough to sweeten the pie, then another layer of pork. Put in ½ pint of white wine, lay some butter on top and close your pie.

If your pie be large it will take a pint of white wine.

The Yorkshire Pork Pie

This recipe is taken from The National Cook Book by Marion Harland and Christine Terhune Herrick, 1896.

Chop **lean pork** somewhat coarsely; butter a **pudding-dish** and line with a good paste; put in the pork interspersed with minced onion and **hard-boiled eggs**, cut into bits and sprinkle with pepper, salt, and **powdered sage**.

Now and then dust with **flour** and drop in a bit of butter.

When all the meat is in, dredge with flour and stick small pieces of **butter** quite thickly all over it.

Cover with puff-paste, cut a slit in the middle of the crust and bake half an hour for each pound of meat.

When it begins to brown, wash the crust with the **white of an egg**. It will give a fine gloss to it.

The **Pie Society** Pie

One of my best selling books was *The Heartbeat Cookbook,* based on the Yorkshire Television series. It was while working on the book that I tasted the modern-day Yorkshire pork pie, and boy can they make pork pies in that neck of the woods! Like the Potts' Lancashire meat pie, they are often known as growlers, although in Halifax they're called stand pies.

In Yorkshire the pork pie is held in such high regard that in 1982 the Pork Pie Appreciation Society was born, and still meets weekly at the Old Bridge Inn at Ripponden. Each week a society member brings a pie to be sampled and assessed by fellow members and given marks out of ten, and there is also an annual national competition to find the best from further afield.

One of the stalwarts of this gathering of the pie-minded is John Green of Wilson's Butchers, and it was to this award-winning pie-maker that I went to have the stunning *Pie Society* pie made. Not only did their creation look awesome, it also tasted brilliant, as 5 families and my publisher can testify, so I owe a huge thank you to John and Wilson's!

For more info visit www.wilsonsbutchers.co.uk.

The Pie Man, Bath

There are two books every British cook and chef should read in their early years to appreciate what a wonderful food heritage we have in this country. The first is *Food in England* by Dorothy Hartley, written in 1954, re-published by Little Brown books in 1999; the second, and my all time favourite, is *Good Things in England* by Florence White, who was the founder of the English Folk Cookery Association. It cost six shillings in 1932 and was re-published by Jonathan Cape in 1972, and again in 1999 by Persephone Books. It is from Florence's book that I give you the following extract:

Mr John Hatton, Spa Director, The Pump Room, Bath sends the following interesting particulars [to Florence White] supplied by an old Bathonian:

The 'Pie Man' stood on the Boro' Walls, between Cater's and Ship and Teagles, close to the pavement by Cater's. He had a brightly polished case of stout tin standing on 4 legs and fitted with three drawers. In one he kept meat pies, the other mince pies, the third had a small charcoal fire arrangement which kept the pies hot.

He announced his presence by fairly quietly repeating quickly, 'All 'ot all 'ot all 'ot' about five times very rapidly. (Try it and you get the effect.) He sold them at the recognized price of the day – one penny each. But with boys, who tossed with him (halfpennies) or with men who tossed (pennies); if they lost he took the money, if they won they had a pie. I think the meat pies were 2d. As the men generally took meat pies, but if they did not choose they had mince pies. But, as I have said, you could also buy.

He disappeared, I think about 1893. I remember him in 1880. As I told Mr. Taylor, he bought stale pies from Fisher's. By stale is meant pies more than a day old. I do not think confectioners are so particular today [1932], but in my youth all confectionary was half price the day after the buns, tarts and pies were made.

This links up the mutton pies of England with the old Nursery rhyme:

'Simple Simon met a pieman going to the Fair,
Says Simple Simon to the pieman "Let me taste your ware."'

Ayrshire Pork & Chicken Pie

900 g / 2 lb pork shoulder,
  Ramsay's Ayrshire if
  possible, ⅓ fat, diced very
  small into 5 mm / ¼ inch
  cubes, skin and gristle
  removed

Generous pinch of salt and
  white pepper

5 ml / 1 teaspoon anchovy
  essence

6 chicken breasts, skin and bone
  removed

2 lb of hot water pastry
  (see recipe on page 36)

1 egg, beaten, to glaze

Pork stock (see recipe on
  page 48)

SERVES 8–10

Pre-heat the oven to 200ºC / 400ºF / gas mark 6.

Combine all the ingredients, except the chicken breasts, in a bowl with two tablespoons of the pork stock.

Make up the hot water pastry and roll it out. Pat two-thirds of it into a lightly greased pie mould or cake tin, about 18 cm / 7 inches in diameter with hinge sides and a detachable base. Evenly distribute to make the pie shape. Reserve the rest of the pastry for the top.

Place the pie case onto a baking tray and put in half the seasoned pork filling. Place the chicken breasts over the pork and then add the remaining pork onto the top of the chicken. Press down and top with the pastry lid. Firmly crimp the edges, being very careful not to break the pie case. Make a hole in the centre of the lid to allow the steam out during the cooking process.

Bake in the lower part of the oven for 2 hours. 10 minutes before the cooking time, egg-glaze the pie and return to the oven.

Once cooking is complete, turn the oven off without opening the door and leave the pie in to dry naturally for 1 hour.

Reheat the pork stock until just warm and pour into the hole of the pie, as much stock as the pie will hold.

Let the pie cool and wrap in cling film, refrigerate for at least 1 day. Take one slice from the pie and hide before letting the family devour your hard work.

When making pork pies, Geo. Watkins anchovy sauce adds a fantastic flavour without making the pie taste at all fishy. It is a bit of a culinary mystery but true!

Raised Pork Pie

(The Cook's Oracle, William Kitchiner 1816)

Make a raised crust, of a good size, with paste . . . about four inches high, take the rind and chine Bone from a Loin of Pork, cut it into chops, beat them with a chopper, season them with pepper and salt and fill your Pie; put on the top and close it, and Pinch it around the edge, rub it over with yolk of egg, and bake it two hours with paper over it, to prevent the crust burning. When done, pour in some good Gravy, with a little ready mixed Mustard (if approved).

N.B. As the above is generally eaten cold, it is an excellent repast for a journey, and will keep for several days.

Pig Pye

'Flea Pyg and cut him in pieces, season with pepper and salt, and nutmeg, and large mace and lay in your coffin good store of raisins and currans, and fill with sweet butter and close it and serve hot or cold.

Veal & Ham Pie

I reckon this wonderful pie, or variations of it, should feature in any really good British party buffet. Known as a gala pie it started life in Norfolk in the seventeenth century. There is nothing nicer than fresh, homemade veal and ham pie, which can be made in a lightly greased and floured 30 cm × 11 cm (12 inches × 4½ inches) bread tin – so you can't use the excuse that you can't find the right pie dish for this monster! Pies such as these were made big because they needed to feed farmer workers out in the fields – a kind of complete ploughman's lunch really – and here is my contribution in picture and recipe form. If I made one for you I'd also give you a slice of egg yolk every time to go with it, just like my Lancashire Pork Pie (see page 58)!

1 kg / 2¼ lb hot water pastry
(see recipe on page 36)

1 kg / 2¼ lb stewing veal

1 kg / 2¼ lb cooked York ham

6 tablespoons roughly chopped
flat-leaf parsley

Grated rind of 1 unwaxed lemon

1 teaspoon mixed herbs

Black pepper

8 large hard-boiled eggs, the
white of the egg trimmed off
before you hit the start of the
yolk

250 ml / 8 fl oz pork stock
(see recipe on page 48)

1 egg, beaten, to glaze

SERVES 8–10

Make up the hot water pastry to the recipe.

Pre-heat the oven to 200°C / 400°F / gas mark 6.

Cut off a third of the pastry and set this aside for the lid and decoration. Flour a board and roll out the rest of the pastry into a large oblong to fit the loaf tin. Let the pastry overhang about 2.5 cm / 1 inch for crimping.

Chop the veal and ham roughly and place into a large bowl, adding the parsley, lemon rind, herbs and pepper. Add 50 ml / 3 tablespoons of the pork stock, mixing thoroughly with your hands. Wash your hands and place half the mixture into the pastry bottom. Carefully place the eggs onto the mixture lengthwise, so each yolk end is touching. Cover the eggs with the rest of the meat mixture, pressing down very gently so that the eggs are not crushed.

Brush the edge of the pastry with the beaten egg and let it rest for 3 minutes. Meanwhile roll out the rest of the pastry to fit the top of the pie. Place the pastry lid on top of the filling and crimp the edges. Trim the pastry and make leaves etc. if you have enough pastry left over. Brush the top of the pie with the beaten egg and make a hole in the centre of the top.

Place the pie on a baking tray and bake in the centre of the oven for 25 minutes. Cover the top of the pie with tin foil and return to the oven, reducing the oven temperature to 160°C / 325°F / gas mark 3 for 95 minutes. Turn off the oven and remove the foil and leave the pie in the oven for a further 10 minutes. Take the pie out and allow it to cool for at least 15 minutes. Poke the hole in the top with a meat skewer and pour in the warm pork stock. Let the pie rest for at least 3 hours and then chill for 24 hours in a fridge. Slice with a sharp knife that has been left in hot water for a few minutes and you will see a yolk every time.

The **Dickinson & Morris** Story

The Melton Mowbray pork pie is a distinct product that is recognisably different from other pork pies, both in physical characteristics and in reputation. It is rich in history and is recognised by consumers as a traditional, regional food product.

The name Dickinson & Morris is synonymous with Melton Mowbray and the delicious pork pies for which the town is famous. The company is the only producer of authentic Melton Mowbray pork pies still based in the centre of this historic Leicestershire market town, at Ye Olde Pork Pie Shoppe on Nottingham Street. The recipe is actually not at all complex; indeed, its very simplicity underlines its authenticity and reminds us that the Melton Mowbray pork pie has remained true to its roots, still being baked without a hoop just as it was the end of the eighteenth century.

Mary Dickinson (1768–1841), a noted pork pie-maker and great grandmother to company founder John Dickonson, is credited with using the first wooden dolly to raise the pastry case, so she is considered to be the originator of the hand-raised Melton Mowbray pork pie.

In 1901, a partnership was formed between John Dickinson and Joseph Morris, who had been taken on as an apprentice in 1886, and the business became Dickinson & Morris. Their thriving pie shop, which was founded in 1851, has become a famous landmark and popular tourist attraction and is now run by renowned pork pie specialist Stephen Hallam. Visitors can not only buy the pies but are also given the opportunity to see a demonstration of how to hand-raise pork pies in the traditional way, and to learn about the history of the pork pie itself. Visit www.porkpie.co.uk for more information.

A ham pye

'Slice some **cold boiled ham** about half an inch thick, make a good **crust**, and thick, over the dish, and lay a layer of ham, shake a little **pepper** over it, then take a **large young fowl** clean plucked, gutted, washed and singed; put a little pepper and salt in the belly, and rub a very little salt on the outside; lay the fowl on the ham, boil some **eggs** hard, put in the yolks, and cover all with ham, then shake some pepper on the ham, and put on a top crust.

Bake it well, have ready when it comes out of the oven some very rich **beef-gravy**, enough to fill the pye, lay on the crust again, and send it to the table hot. A fresh ham will not be so tender; so that I always boil my ham one day, and bring it to the table, and make a pye of it. It does better than an unboiled ham. If you put two large fowls in they will make a fine pye.
But that is according to your company, more or less.

The crust must be the same you make for venison pasty. You should pour a little strong gravy into the pye when you bake it, just to bake the meat, and then fill it up when it comes out of the oven. Boil some truffles and morels, and put into the pye, it is a great addition; and fresh mushrooms or dried ones'.

The London Cook: or the whole art of cookery made easy and familiar (1762),
by William Gelleroy, cook to her Grace the Duchess of Argyle.

Egg, Bacon & Sausage Criss-cross Pie

This is a very tasty picnic bake which can be served hot or cold, and is very nice served with homemade or traditional ginger beer.

350 g / 12 oz ready made shortcrust pastry

3 large hard-boiled eggs, shelled

8 rashers lean, rindless streaky or back bacon, grilled

225 g / 8 oz Cumberland sausage meat or sausages skin removed

2 eggs, beaten with 150 ml / 5 fl oz milk

Salt and black pepper

SERVES 6

Pre-heat the oven to 200°C / 400°F / gas mark 6.

Roll out two-thirds of the pastry and line a buttered pie dish or deep plate.

Bake blind for 15 minutes and allow the pastry to cool.

Slice the eggs and chop the bacon and place those ingredients with small pieces of the sausage meat scattered around the pastry case. Pour over the egg and milk mixture, retaining a little to glaze.

Season the pie mixture contents.

Roll out the remaining pastry and cut into thin strips about ½ inch wide and lay them across the pie to make a criss cross pattern on the pie, sealing well all around the edges. Glaze with the remaining egg and milk mixture.

Bake in the centre of the oven for 10 minutes, then reduce the heat to 180°C / 350°F / gas mark 4 for a further 25 minutes.

Look what I made with the leftovers!

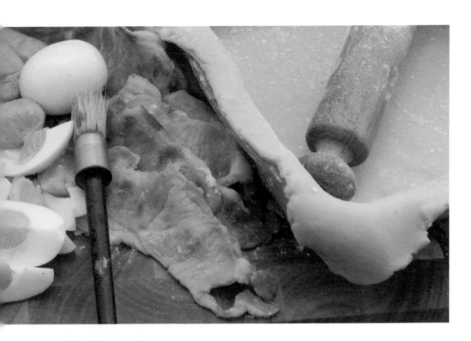

Huntsman Pie

A true taste of Yorkshire from John Green, a master pie baker and partner at Wilsons Butchers. I asked John for a recipe, but it would be too long and time consuming to make it to the Wilsons' standard, so here's my simplified version. The sweetness of the stuffing complements the savoury pork and the moist turkey meat beautifully – and don't panic, it's OK here to use a good-quality packet stuffing if you can't make it from scratch!

Apple and Apricot Stuffing

75 g / 3 oz butter

2 onions, finely chopped

2 Bramley apples, peeled, cored and cut into small cubes

1 tablespoon lemon juice and zest

75 g / 3 oz dried apricots diced

450 g / 1 lb dried breadcrumbs

3 ml / ¾ teaspoon dried thyme

5 ml / 1 teaspoon chopped parsley

Salt and black pepper

Freshly grated nutmeg

150 ml / 5 fl oz pork stock

75 ml / 3 fl oz apple juice

Stuffing

Melt the butter in a pan, add the onions and cook gently until they have softened (about 5 minutes). Remove from the heat and allow to cool. Add and mix in all the rest of the ingredients. Cook slowly for 10 minutes, stirring all the time. Season as necessary and place to one side until required.

Pie Ingredients

450 g / 1 lb turkey thigh meat, skin and bone removed

600 ml / 1 pint chicken stock

1 kg / 2¼ lb of pork shoulder, ⅓ fat, diced very small into 5 mm / ¼ inch cubes, skin and gristle removed

Generous pinch of salt and white pepper

5 ml / 1 teaspoon anchovy essence

Pork stock (see recipe on page 48)

1 egg, beaten, to glaze

SERVES 8–10

Filling

Put the chicken stock into a large saucepan, add the turkey meat and simmer slowly for 45 to 55 minutes until the meat is tender.

Carefully remove the turkey meat and place to one side and allow to cool.

Pre-heat the oven to 200°C / 400°F / gas mark 6.

Combine the pork, salt, pepper and anchovy essence, together with a little pork stock to moisten, in a bowl. Make up the hot water pastry as described on page 36.

Roll out the pastry and pat two-thirds into a lightly greased pie mould or cake tin about 20 cm / 8 inches in diameter with hinged sides and a detachable base. Evenly distribute the pastry to make the pie shape. Reserve the rest of the pastry for the top.

Place the pie case onto a baking tray and put in the seasoned pork filling. Put the turkey meat over the pork filling, then top with the fruit stuffing. Press everything down carefully and finally top with the pastry lid.

Firmly crimp the edges, being very careful not to break the pie case. Make a hole in the centre of the lid to allow the steam out during the cooking process.

Bake in the lower part of the oven for 2 hours. 10 minutes before the cooking time, egg-glaze the pie and return to the oven.

Reheat the pork stock until just warm and pour into the hole of the pie, as much stock as the pie will hold.

Let the pie cool, wrap in cling film and refrigerate for at least 24 hours.

Cheshire Pork & Bramley Apple Pie with Cheese Pastry

300 g / 11 oz Cheddar cheese pastry (see recipe on page 41)

1 kg / 2¼ lb lean pork, minced

2 slices naturally cured, unsmoked bacon, minced

1 tablespoon chopped sage leaves

Grated nutmeg

Salt and black pepper

4 Bramley apples, peeled, cored and sliced

275 ml / ½ pint dry white wine

75 g / 3 oz butter

1 egg, beaten, to glaze

SERVES 8–10

Roll out the pastry and line a 20 cm / 8 inch pie dish. Reserve enough for the lid.

Season the pork and bacon with the sage, nutmeg, salt and pepper and arrange in alternate layers with the apples, sprinkling the apples with a little sugar if desired, and finishing off with pork and bacon layer.

Moisten with white wine and dot with butter.

Add the pastry lid, decorate, and cut a slit in the top.

Glaze and bake at 220°C / 425°F / gas mark 7 for 15 minutes, then reduce the heat to 190°C / 375°F / gas mark 5 and bake for a further 25 minutes.

The British do grow the best baking apples in Europe!

'Likky' Pie

This feast-day dish, more accurately known as Leek Pie, has a delicate, creamy flavour.

225 g / 8 oz leeks, trimmed,
sliced and washed

450 g / 1 lb lean boneless pork,
cut into 2.5 cm / 1 inch
cubes

Salt and black pepper

150 ml / ¼ pint fresh milk

75 ml / 3 fl oz fresh single cream

2 eggs, lightly beaten

250 g / 9 oz puff pastry
(see recipe on page 39)

SERVES 4–6

Parboil the leeks in salted water for about 5 minutes. Drain well. Fill a 1.2 litre / 2 pint pie dish with the leeks and pork. Season to taste and pour in the milk.

Cover with foil and bake at 200°C / 400°F / gas mark 6 for about 1 hour (don't worry if it looks curdled).

Stir the cream into the eggs, and then pour into the dish. Allow the pie to cool.

Roll out the pastry on a lightly floured surface to 5 cm / 2 inches wider than the dish. Cut a 2.5 cm / 1 inch strip from the outer edge and use to line the dampened rim of the pie dish. Dampen the pastry rim with water, cover with the pastry lid and seal the edges well, pressing a pattern into them if you wish. Make a hole in the centre of the pie and use any pastry trimmings to decorate.

Bake at 220°C / 425°F / gas mark 7 for about 25–30 minutes, until risen and golden brown.

Beef

It really is hard to beat a good bit of British beef. The quality is high, the choices huge; it is sustainable and readily available, and by buying it you are supporting our hardworking farmers. I strongly believe that there is no need to buy beef that originates from anywhere else in the world, and somehow it just seems plain wrong to fill such British favourites as steak and kidney pie or meat and potato pie with anything else!

I buy my meat from traditional butchers or direct from the farmer wherever possible, or from the now hugely popular stalls that enrich and enliven our market halls and streets. You can buy it in supermarkets too, of course, where I must admit that the standard these days is often very good, and the packaging tells you where the meat is from. There are also some excellent online shops which are a particularly good way of sourcing beef from other regions or for more specialist produce, such as free range, organic or matured beef.

This chapter is jam-packed with the kind of recipes that truly define traditional British cooking.

Lancashire Rump Steak Pan Pie

A good friend of mine, Peter Smith, used to make this pie for his customers at the Cross Gates pub in Blacko, near Burnley. Peter used a Cheshire cheese pastry topping instead of suet and he always served this with minted peas and warm wholemeal crusty cobs with lashings of butter. Wonderful!

450 g / 1 lb rump steak

1 large onion, sliced

2 carrots, diced

1 small turnip, diced

Pinch of English mustard powder

Salt and black pepper

450 g / 1 lb King Edward potatoes, diced

600 ml / 1 pint beef stock

Pete's suet pastry

100 g / 4 oz flour

50 g / 2 oz suet, grated

1.5 ml / ¼ teaspoon baking powder

1 pinch of salt

Water

SERVES 8–10

Cut the meat into cubes and put them into a casserole dish with the stock. Add the onion, carrots and turnip to the pan with the seasoning. Simmer for 1 hour.

Add the potatoes and cook for a further 15 minutes.

Make the pastry by combining the flour, suet, baking powder and salt and mixing to a dough with the water. Roll out the pastry and cover the top of the filling with it.

Put the lid on and simmer for half an hour until the pastry is done.

Brown the top under the grill before serving in the pan.

Beefsteak & Ale Pie

This is one of the most popular pies in Britain, and few pub and restaurant menus are without their own version. It was a favourite at the award-winning Sharrow Bay Country House Hotel in the Lake District, where I did some filming several years ago with proprietors Brian Sack and Francis Coulson – it was superb chef Francis who invented 'sticky toffee pudding'!

I am always being asked for the perfect pub recipe for this pie, so here's my offering. I always use locally sourced chuck beef and lamb kidneys, and serve with real hand-made chips, minted peas, and some lovely fresh crusty bread to dunk in the juices. Being a northern lad, I use a very well known Lancashire beer, but I'll allow you to use something from your neck of the woods if you insist!

450 g / 1 lb ready to use
    puff pastry

25 g / 1 oz beef dripping

675 g / 1½ lb chuck steak, cut
    into chunks, fat removed

225 g / 8 oz lamb's kidney, diced

2 large red onions, finely
    chopped

40 g / 1½ oz plain flour

nutmeg, grated

425 ml / 15 fl oz rich beef stock

75 ml / 3 fl oz bitter

1 tablespoon chopped parsley

Salt and black pepper

1 teaspoon lemon juice

SERVES 4–6

In a large non-stick saucepan or casserole, heat the dripping and fry the steak for 4 minutes. Add the kidney and onions, cook for a further 2 minutes. Sprinkle with flour and nutmeg and cook for 3 minutes more then add the beef stock, bitter, lemon juice, seasoning and parsley and simmer for 60 minutes. Allow the steak to cool completely and place into a pie casserole or large pie dish.

Pre-heat the oven to 200°C / 400°F / gas mark 6.

On a floured board, roll out 1 sheet of puff pastry dough until it is 1 inch larger on all sides than the top of the beef dish, leaving enough dough to make a 1-inch strip. Brush the strip with egg and lay it, egg side down, on top of the casserole or pie dish. Without stretching, press the strip onto the rim and outside edge of the dish. Using a knife, cut the remaining sheet of pastry and top the pie, using any leftover pastry to decorate, sticking the shapes to the lid with beaten egg.

Place the pie on a baking sheet and bake in the centre of the oven for 35 minutes. Remove the baked pie from oven and let it rest for 10 minutes before serving.

Pippa's Perfect Pie

I do like people who are prepared to have a go at baking, even if they are not perfect at it. Every year I host two major food festivals in the North West, at Wigan and Southport, and for the past three years I have had a young fan who will taste anything I cook. Her name is Pippa Hardy and she offered me a recipe she makes which her mother, Mo, taught her. So here is Pippa's top-notch steak and kidney creation – enjoy!

450 g / 1 lb lean English braising steak, cut into 2.5 cm / 1 inch cubes

15 ml / 1 tablespoon sunflower oil

1 onion, peeled and sliced

100 g / 4 oz chestnut mushrooms, quartered

225 g / 8 oz ox kidney, cored and cut into small chunks

15 ml / 1 tablespoon plain flour

450 ml / ¾ pint good, hot beef stock

1 sachet bouquet garni

200 ml / 7 fl oz stout

Salt and black pepper

500 g / 1 lb 2 oz shortcrust pastry (see recipe on page 33)

1 egg, beaten, to glaze

SERVES 4–6

Heat the oil in a large casserole dish and cook the beef for 3–4 minutes until brown.

Add the onion and mushrooms and cook for 4–5 minutes until coloured. Add the kidneys and cook for 1–2 minutes. Sprinkle over the flour.

Add the stock, bouquet garni, stout and seasoning. Bring to the boil, reduce the heat, cover and cook for 2 hours until the meat is tender. Remove the bouquet garni and spoon the mixture into four 300 ml / ½ pint individual pie dishes.

Pre-heat the oven to 190°C / 375°F / gas mark 5.

Roll out the pastry and cut out four lids, 1 cm / ½ inch larger than the surface of each dish. Dampen the edges of each dish with a little water and place the pastry lid on top of the meat filling.

Trim off any excess pastry and lightly press the edges to seal. Brush with beaten egg and bake for 35–40 minutes until the pastry is golden.

Pippa says serve with fat chips and seasonal vegetables or salad

Victorian Corned Beef Hash

Corned beef is traditionally made by curing brisket in large grains – or 'corns' – of salt, and the tinned version was created to provide field rations for the army from the Boer War to the Second World War. For this wonderful recipe from yesteryear I use a good piece of brisket, boned and rolled. There is nothing nicer and it's far better than using canned corned beef.

This is a real classic and an excellent winter warmer, traditionally served with buttered spring cabbage and English mustard. You can do two versions of the topping: one with just sliced potatoes sprinkled with shavings of frozen butter for a crisp topping; the second with both butter and cheese. I love the latter but my mother hates cheese so I always do the plain version for her. I also use this recipe for corned beef hash pasties and they taste sensational too.

1.4 kg / 3 lb boned and rolled brisket

50 g / 2 oz butter

20 shallots, peeled

4 large potatoes, peeled and quartered

2 large carrots, peeled and cut into chunks

2 parsnips, peeled and cut into chunks

1 small turnip, peeled and chopped

1 sprig of fresh thyme

1 sprig of rosemary

Salt and black pepper

1 litre beef stock

15 ml / 1 tablespoon flour

15 ml / 1 tablespoon butter

450 g / cooked sliced potatoes

SERVES 6–8

Pre-heat the oven to 275°F / 140°C / gas mark 1.

Quickly fry the beef off in the butter, browning it well all over, then place to one side.

Fry the shallots, potatoes, carrots, parsnip and turnip in the butter and beef juice. Then place the beef, surrounded by the vegetables into a large deep casserole/pot. Add the herbs and the stock, seasoning well, and cover with a lid or cooking foil and place into the centre of the oven. Cook for 3 hours.

Drain the vegetables and mash with butter. Shred and dice the beef and blend with the vegetable mash thoroughly. Bring the stock juices to the boil and reduce by a third, removing the herbs afterwards.

Blend the flour and butter to a paste, add to the beef stock and whisk until the sauce thickens. Adjust the seasoning and pour the sauce into a deep earthenware pie dish, or individual pie dishes. Add the hash, top with sliced potatoes and dot with butter or sprinkle 75 g of your favourite cheese on the top. Place in the oven at 200°C / 400°F / gas mark 6 for 20 minutes and serve with homemade piccalilli (see recipe on page 237).

Steak & Cowheel Pie

This sounds like real Desperate Dan stuff, doesn't it! Though some may be squeamish about it, cowheel is a great source of gelatine and gives a wonderful flavour to pies. Your local butcher can always source it for you, and many town market stalls will sell it too.

1 lb 6 oz shortcrust pastry
  (see page 33)

25 g / 1 oz beef dripping

700 g / 1 lb 8 oz chuck steak, cut
  into chunks, fat removed

275 g / 10 oz cowheel meat,
  diced

14 shallots or 2 large onions

40 g / 1½ oz plain flour

425 ml / 15 fl oz meat stock
  (see page 47)

75 ml / 3 fl oz red wine

1 tablespoon chopped parsley

Salt and pepper

1 teaspoon lemon juice

1 egg yolk, beaten, to glaze

SERVES 4–6

In a large non-stick saucepan or casserole heat the dripping and fry the steak for 4 minutes. Add the cowheel and shallots or onions, cook for a further 2 minutes. Sprinkle with flour and nutmeg and cook for 3 minutes, adding the meat stock, red wine, lemon juice, parsley and seasoning and simmering for a further 50 minutes. Allow the steak and cowheel to cool completely and place into a large pie dish.

Pre-heat the oven to 200°C / 400°F / gas mark 6.

Roll out the pastry on a floured surface, using two thirds for the base and the rest for the topping. Grease and line a pie dish with the pastry.

Place the steak and cowheel into the lined pie dish and top with the remaining pastry, and glaze.

Bake in the oven for 25 minutes, then lower the temperature to 180°C / 350°F / gas mark 4 and bake for a further 20 minutes until the crust is lovely and golden.

The G.S. Family Meat Pie

A dear old friend of mine, George Saint, sent me this recipe that he made for his customers when he had a pub in Wembley with his wife Fran. They looked after me after a hard day's night when I was chef at Wembley Stadium and Arena. Thanks again, you two!

50 g / 2 oz butter

1 onion diced

1 carrot, diced

1 small turnip, diced

370 g / 13 oz lean English minced beef

225 g / 8 oz Cumberland sausage meat

15 ml / 1 tablespoon plain flour

190 ml / 6.6 fl oz meat stock (see recipe on page 47)

Salt and black pepper

350 g / 12 oz shortcrust pastry (see recipe on page 33)

1 egg yolk, beaten, to glaze

SERVES 4–6

Melt the butter in a large saucepan and gently fry the chopped vegetables for about 10 minutes. Add the mince and sausage meat, cook until they are brown, stirring occasionally.

Add the flour and stir well. Add the stock and bring to the boil and let it simmer for 10 minutes.

Season to taste and allow the pie mixture to cool.

Make up the pastry. Line a 25 cm / 10-inch pie dish with two thirds of the pastry, add the cooled mixture and cover with remaining pastry and glaze.

Cook in a pre-heated oven at 200°C / 400°F / gas mark 6 for 35 to 40 minutes.

Porters' Steak, Guinness & Mushroom Pie

If you have never been to Porters in Covent Garden, then you are missing a *Pie Society* experience. Richard Bridgeman, the owner, gave me this recipe and it is still the all-time favourite pie at Porters. Take a look at my steak and kidney pudding recipe on page 160 for the story of how Richard came to own this wonderful English eatery.

2 medium onions, 1 finely chopped, 1 thinly sliced

25 g / 1 oz butter

700 g / 1½ lb chuck steak, cut into 4 cm / 1½ inch cubes

50 g / 2 oz seasoned flour

1 dessertspoon sunflower oil

150 ml / ¼ pint Guinness (or red wine)

300 ml / ½ pint beef stock

1 sachet bouquet garni

Salt and black pepper

275 g / 10 oz button mushrooms

275 g / 10 oz puff pastry

1 egg, beaten, to glaze

SERVES 4–6

Melt the butter in a casserole dish, add the onions and cook gently for 10 minutes, until soft and golden brown. Remove from the dish and put to one side.

Toss the steak in the seasoned flour, patting off the excess. Add the oil to the casserole dish, increase the heat and brown the meat in batches of 6 / 8 cubes at a time. Drain the excess oil from the dish. Return onions and steak to the casserole, increase the heat and add the Guinness (or wine), bring to the boil and continue to boil for 1 minute.

Add the stock, bouquet garni, salt and pepper, return to boil, cover and then place in the oven, 170°C / 325°F / gas mark 3 for 90 minutes. Add the mushrooms and cook for a further 1–1½ hours or until the steak is extremely tender. Check the seasoning, remove the bouquet garni and allow to cool. For maximum flavour this process is best done the night before. Store in the refrigerator, but remove 1 hour before baking.

When ready to cook the pie, pre-heat the oven to 220°C / 425°F / gas mark 7. Spoon the steak mixture into a 1.2 litre / 2 pint pie dish. Roll out the pastry slightly larger than the pie dish. Moisten the rim of the dish and place the pastry on top, sealing the edges well. Cut away the excess pastry and firmly crimp the edges. Brush with beaten egg and cook for 30–40 minutes until the pastry is crisp and golden brown.

Gallimore's Steak & Guinness Pie

I went into Gallimore's restaurant in Wigan to see my old friend Howard Gallimore and to taste his St Patrick's Day special. It was full of the flavours of Ireland, and his pastry chef Melissa made an exceptional job of a butter crust pastry.

450 g / 1 lb rich shortcrust pastry (see recipe on page 33)

25 g / 1 oz beef dripping

675 g / 1½ lb rump steak, cut into chunks, fat removed

225 g / 8 oz lamb's kidney, diced

2 large red onions, finely chopped

40 g / 1½ oz plain flour

Nutmeg, grated

½ teaspoon thyme

425 ml / 15 fl oz rich beef stock

100 ml / 4 fl oz Guinness

1 tablespoon chopped parsley

Salt and black pepper

1 teaspoon lemon juice

SERVES 4–6

In a large non-stick saucepan or casserole, heat the dripping and fry the steak for 4 minutes, add the kidney and onion, cook for a further 2 minutes. Sprinkle with flour and nutmeg and cook for another 3 minutes, add the beef stock, Guinness, lemon juice, herbs, seasoning and parsley and simmer for 60 minutes. Allow to cool completely and place into a pie casserole or large pie dish.

Pre-heat the oven to 200ºC / 400ºF / gas mark 6.

On a floured board, roll out the pastry until it is 1 inch larger on all sides than the top of the pie dish, leaving enough dough to make a 1-inch strip. Brush the strip with egg and lay it, egg down, on top of the casserole or pie dish. Without stretching, press dough onto rim and outside edge of dish. Using a knife, cut remaining sheet of pastry and top the pie, using any leftover pastry to for decorative shapes. Place the pie on a baking sheet and bake in the centre of the oven for 35 minutes. Remove the baked pie from the oven and let it rest for 10 minutes before serving.

Devon Huntsman Meat Pie

There are so many varieties of the pies which were handed out to the huntsman before they set off on a cold day's horse riding. This is nothing like Leeds-based Wilsons' huntsman pie and completely different from a Scottish huntsman pie, which would have used venison instead of beef with a potato and swede topping. One of the nicest pies I tasted on a visit to Wales was from Edwards of Conwy. Their huntsman pie is the current Welsh champion cold eating pie, judged by Meat Promotion Wales at last year's Royal Welsh Show. It is produced in individual as well as one pound family sizes and is made from shoulder pork and turkey, with an open top covered with herb and onion stuffing. Well worth tracking down, I can tell you!

450 g / 1 lb lean mince beef

900 g / 2 lb potatoes diced

2 onions, peeled and sliced

2 large Bramley cooking apples, cored and sliced

275 ml / ½ pint beef stock

Salt and black pepper

Pinch of nutmeg

200 g / 7 oz shortcrust pastry

1 egg, beaten, to glaze

SERVES 4–6

Season the minced beef and alternate layers of mince, potato, onion and apple.

Pour over the beef stock, add the nutmeg and then put the pastry lid on. Decorate, cut a slit in the top, and glaze.

Bake at 220°C / 425°F / mark 7 for 15 minutes, then reduce the heat to 190°C / 375°F / mark 5 and bake for a further 35 minutes.

Have a go using a different meat than beef; pork and mutton would be a great combination

Classic Scotch Beef & Haggis in Puff Pastry

I devised this recipe for a Taste of Scotland cookery demonstration at a BBC Good Food Show at the NEC, using my friend John Fallon's haggis – look out for Grants canned haggis in supermarkets.

900 g / 2 lb fillet of Aberdeen
    Angus beef

Salt and black pepper

75 g / 3 oz butter

2 large red onions finely
    chopped

175 g / 6 oz wild mushrooms

450 g / 1 lb puff pastry

175 g / 6 oz Grants canned
    haggis, warmed

1 egg, beaten, to glaze

SERVES 6–8

With a sharp knife, trim the fat from the beef fillet. Season the meat well with salt and pepper.

Melt the butter in a large frying pan and add the fillet, sealing the meat all over, cooking for at least 6 minutes. Remove the beef from the pan, placing it to one side to cool.

In the same pan add a little more butter and the chopped onion and mushrooms, cooking until all the moisture has evaporated. Season well and allow to cool.

Pre-heat the oven to 200ºC / 400ºF / gas mark 6.

Roll out the pastry into a large rectangle and place onto a greased baking sheet. Spread the onion and mushroom mixture onto the centre of the pastry, then place the beef onto the mixture. Top the fillet with a layer of warm haggis and then chill for 30 minutes.

Take out of the fridge and brush the edges of the pastry with the beaten egg, then fold the pastry over the filling, pressing the edges together to seal the pastry. Make flowers and leaves from any leftover pastry, and glaze the top of the pie.

Bake in the centre of the oven for 20 minutes, then reduce the oven to 180ºC / 350ºF / gas mark 4 for a further 15 minutes until golden brown. Allow to rest for 5 minutes before serving with Madeira sauce and a horseradish mash.

My Pop's Beef Mince & Potato Pie with Bury Black Pudding

I was given a challenge by Granada Television to make a meal for under a fiver to feed a family of four, so I created one with weather presenter Fred Talbot. This is my new version, updated to feed six.

25 g / 1 oz beef dripping

1 kg / 2¼ lb lean minced beef

900 g / 2 lb potatoes, peeled and diced

150 g / 5 oz diced carrot

225 g / 8 oz sliced onion

1 tablespoon mixed herbs

25 g / 1 oz plain flour

100 g / 4 oz marrowfat peas

1 teaspoon Worcestershire sauce

300 ml / ½ pint beef stock

Salt and black pepper

225 g / 8 oz real Lancashire black pudding, skin removed and diced

450 g / 1 lb shortcrust pastry

1 egg, beaten, to glaze

SERVES 6

Pre-heat the oven to 200°C / 400°F / gas mark 6.

Heat the dripping in a large saucepan until it is quite hot, add the mince and very quickly seal and brown it for 3 minutes, add the potatoes, carrot, onion and mixed herbs, cooking for 2 minutes, then sprinkle with the flour. Stir, add the peas, Worcestershire sauce and beef stock. Bring to the boil slowly and remove from the heat. Season well and taste. Put the mixture into a 1.2 litre / 2 pint pie dish, scattering the diced black pudding over the top (this helps to thicken the pie during the cooking process).

Roll out the pastry and cover the pie dish, sealing and crimping the pastry all around. Trim off any excess pastry and use it to decorate the top and then glaze.

Brush with egg and bake in the centre of the oven for 45 minutes.

Serve with baked beans, bread and butter.

FRESH
MEATY
Pork Ribs
£3.30 /kg
£1.50 lb
NOT FROZEN
FRESH

Cottage Pie

It is very important that you use the best lean mince for this glorious pie, teamed with a creamy buttered mash – you can even add a little horseradish sauce to the mash for that extra kick.

25 g / 1 oz beef dripping

450 g / 1 lb roughly minced beef

225 g / 8 oz rump steak, diced

1 large onion, skinned and sliced

1 large carrot, peeled and diced

A pinch of fresh thyme

Salt and black pepper

25 g / 1 oz plain flour

300 ml / ½ pint beef stock

1 tablespoon Worcestershire sauce

1 tablespoon tomato puree

700 g / 1½ lb warm mashed potato, seasoned and buttered

25 g / 1 oz butter, softened

SERVES 4–6

Pre-heat the oven to 200°C / 400°F / gas mark 6.

Melt the dripping in a large saucepan and fry the mince and steak for 10 minutes, then add the onion, carrot and thyme. Fry for a further 5 minutes, season with salt and pepper.

Add the flour and cook for a further 2 minutes, very slowly add the beef stock, and finally add the Worcestershire sauce and tomato puree and cook for a 25 minutes more, stirring every 4 minutes.

Allow the mixture to cool then place it into a deep pie dish and cover with warm mashed potato, using a fork to spread the potato, ensuring every area is completely covered.

Sprinkle with softened butter and bake in the centre of the oven for 25 minutes.

The **Denby Dale** Pie

There is a famous 220-year-old tradition associated with Denby Dale in Yorkshire, one that has put the place firmly on the national and international map as The Pie Village. But these are no ordinary meat pies; these are monster meat – and sometimes potato too – pies that have been registered in the *Guinness Book of Records* in past years!

The first recorded making of a pie in the village was in 1788 to celebrate the recovery of King George III from mental illness. Since that time nine other pies have been baked, usually to coincide with a special event (such as the Battle of Waterloo, and victory in World War I), or to raise money for a good cause. Beef is the main meat used, but definitely no game after the Queen Victoria Jubilee pie debacle in 1887, when the result was inedible (see pages 15–16)!

The most recent outsize pie was baked for the Millennium in 2000. The pie dish weighed 12 tonnes, and measured 40 ft by 8 ft by 44 inches deep. It was divided into 24 compartments, each heated by its own individually controlled, 3 kilowatt heating element. The contents included 5000 kg British beef (provided by ASDA), 2000 kg potatoes and 1000 kg onions. And, for the first time, 100 litres of John Smith's Best Bitter.

On Pie Day, the 2nd September, the fully cooked pie was drawn on a seventy-foot long wagon through the village and into the Pie field, where the Bishop of Wakefield blessed it. Around 30,000 people came to the event and watched former cricket umpire Dickie Bird cut the pie.

In 2001, Janet Purcell, a chef with a penchant for making pies, established the Denby Dale Pie Company with friends. Their aim was to make quality pies with fresh local produce and prime cuts of beef, and using limited mechanisation. The pies are sold uncooked, so that the consumer can experience a really freshly baked taste. Visit www.denbydalepiecompany.co.uk for more information.

Lamb & mutton

Lamb is naturally tender meat with a distinctive flavour, and interestingly it is lower in saturated fat than many other red meats. Although the word lamb is used to refer to all sheep meat, there are in fact three different types: lamb itself is from animals which are less than one year old; hogget is from one- to two-year-old sheep; and mutton is the meat of sheep that are over two years old. Mutton has slightly richer flavour and you really need to cook the meat at a slightly lower temperature for longer to get the ideal mix of texture, tenderness and taste. Lamb, hogget and/or mutton are available throughout most of the year, except for two or three months in the winter when the animals go through a 'store' period.

Although most of the recipes in this chapter use mutton you can replace it with lamb or hogget – you may need to reduce the cooking time, though lamb is often best cooked long and slow too. But I'm going to get on my soap box again and really encourage you to seek out mutton. It's well worth the effort for the taste alone, but if you remember that by buying it you'll be helping British sheep farmers too, that makes it doubly good. Have a read of some of the Mutton Renaissance Campaign stuff. I'm always trying to win converts to the cause! (www.muttonrenaissance.org)

Renaissance Mutton Shepherd's Pie

I've lost count of the number of arguments I have had over this pie, and if I had a pint for every time, I would own a brewery: shepherd's pie is made with mutton, hogget or lamb, and cottage pie with beef. So there!

I do feel that the meat must be cooked for a shepherd's pie, and that is the first stage. I have also added extra flavours because I have found the original recipes to be very bland, including Mrs Beeton's from 1861. I get my mutton from a very reputable supplier called Choice Cuts in Bolton market because it is bred locally and does not travel hundreds of miles. Take the time to search out your nearest supplier who operates in the same way – investigate your local markets, or try visiting www.muttonrenaissance.org/shopping.

25 g / 1 oz beef dripping

450 g / 1 lb roughly minced mutton

225 g / 8 oz loin mutton, fat removed and diced

2 large onions, skinned and sliced

2 carrots, peeled and diced

1 teaspoon of fresh rosemary, chopped

Salt and black pepper

25 g / 1 oz plain flour

300 ml / 10 fl oz mutton or lamb stock

2 tablespoons port

1 tablespoon Worcestershire sauce

1 tablespoon tomato puree

100 g / 4 oz sweet peas

700 g / 1½ lb warm mashed potato, seasoned and buttered

25 g / 1 oz butter, softened

1 teaspoon freshly crushed rosemary

75 g / 3 oz crumbled Lancashire cheese (optional)

SERVES 4–6

Pre-heat the oven to 200ºC / 400ºF / gas mark 6.

Melt the dripping in a large saucepan and fry the mutton or lamb for 10 minutes, add the onions, carrots and rosemary, fry for a further 5 minutes, season with salt and pepper.

The Lancashire cheese is optional but highly recommended

Add the flour and cook for a further 2 minutes, then very slowly add the stock and port. Finally add the Worcestershire sauce and tomato puree and cook for a further 25 minutes, stirring every 4 minutes. Mix in the peas and allow the mixture to cool.

Place the mixture into a deep pie dish and cover with warm mashed potato, using a fork to spread the potato, ensuring that all the meat is completely covered.

Sprinkle with softened butter, crushed rosemary and the crumbled Lancashire cheese.

Bake in the centre of the oven for 20 minutes and serve with warm beetroot, carrots, turnip and mustard sauce.

'The word about mutton is starting to get around. Smart chefs are already putting it on their menus, and a few enlightened butchers are beginning to market it as something rather special.'

In 2004, His Royal Highness the Prince of Wales launched the Mutton Renaissance, a campaign to return this wonderful, much-underrated meat to our dinner plates and help Britain's family farmers in the process. Several years ago I wrote the biography of William Kitchiner, whose book *The Housekeeper's Oracle,* sparked my interest in the use of mutton. There is some disagreement about the exact definition of mutton, but my fellow mutton fan Hugh Fearnley-Whittingstall offers a good one:

> Sheep farming experts generally agree that mutton refers to meat from sheep that are over two years old (lamb meat is generally from animals that have been reared for five months). Traditionalists argue that mutton is always the meat from a wether (a wether is a castrated male sheep; it is thought that castration improves the taste of some meats). A more contemporary view is that mutton comes from a breeding ewe that has reached the end of its productive life. According to William Kitchiner in The *Housekeeper's Oracle* (1817), the finest mutton came from a five-year-old wether.

One of the best producers of mutton is Ben Weatherall's Blackface Meat Company based in south-west Scotland, which I have visited several times. Ben's delicious, sustainably produced meat is a real treat and can be bought by visiting www.blackface.co.uk. And at the other end of the country, in Devon, Richard and Barbara Barker produce beautiful mutton and other meats on the Fowlescombe Estate, all available online at www.fowlescombe.co.uk.

Mutton & Turnip Pie

This recipe is from Mark Hix, renowned master chef and director of The Ivy. I do admire talent, and Mark is at the top of the tree with this corker of a pie – thanks Mark (and Quadrille Publishing) for allowing me to reproduce it here.

The filling for this simple pie is slow-cooked to help the flavours of the mutton and the vegetables combine. Serve on a cold day with buttered cabbage, boiled potatoes or mashed swede and enjoy with a fruity red wine.

1 kg / 2¼ lb neck fillet of mutton, cut into rough 2 cm / ¾ inch pieces

Salt and black pepper

Plain flour for dusting

Vegetable oil for frying

2 large onions, peeled and finely chopped

A small sprig of rosemary

1.4 litres / 2½ pints chicken or lamb stock

450 g / 1 lb turnips, peeled and cut into rough 2–3 cm / 1 inch chunks

350 g / 12 oz puff pastry, rolled to about 1 cm / ½ inch thick

1 egg, beaten, to glaze

SERVES 4–6

Pre-heat the oven to 200°C / 400°F / gas mark 6.

Season the pieces of mutton and dust generously with about a tablespoon or so of flour.

Heat the vegetable oil in a heavy-bottomed saucepan and fry the pieces of mutton and the onions without colouring them too much, about 3–4 minutes.

Add the rosemary and stock, bring to the boil and simmer gently for about 1½–2 hours until the mutton is soft and tender.

Add the turnips. Cover with a lid and add a little boiled water if necessary. Simmer for about 15 minutes until the turnips are cooked. Remove from heat and leave to cool.

Meanwhile cut the pastry a little larger than the pie dish, or dishes if you are making individual pies. When the mutton mixture is cooled transfer it to your pie dish. Brush the edges of the pastry with some egg and lay the pastry on the dish, pressing the edges onto the rim. Cut a slit about 2–3 cms (1 inch) in the centre to let the steam out, or for a larger pie use a pie funnel.

Bake the pie for 40–45 minutes until golden.

Hogget or Mutton Pie à la Reform

I have based this recipe on the Alexis Soyer classic, Lamb Cutlet Reform, which he made for the Reform Club in London. I created this version for the BBC when I was filming the Victorian Roadshow in Beamish in 2001, because hogget and mutton were staple Victorian meats.

8 loin of hogget or mutton steaks, bone removed

50 g / 2 oz York ham, chopped

50 g / 2 oz mushrooms, chopped

Pinch each of thyme and nutmeg

Salt and pepper

150 ml / ¼ pint of hot mutton stock, thickened with flour and butter

60 ml / 4 tablespoons claret

60 ml / 4 tablespoons redcurrant jelly

200 g / 7 oz shortcrust pastry (see recipe on page 33)

1 egg, beaten, to glaze

SERVES 4–6

Lightly brown the steaks on each side in a little butter. Lay them in a deep pie dish and sprinkle with ham and mushrooms. Season with nutmeg, thyme, salt and pepper, and.

Pour the hot stock over the meat and stir in the claret and redcurrant jelly. Allow to cool.

Roll out the pastry and cover the pie dish, crimp and-glaze.

Bake the pie at 220ºC / 425ºF / gas mark 7 for 10 minutes and then reduce the heat to 170–180ºC / 325–350ºF / gas mark 3–4 for a further 40 minutes.

Cumberland Sweet Mutton & Guinness, or 'Best of British', Pie

This is a happy handshake between the English Lakes and Eire, savoury and sweet, and I gave it to Manchester tenor Russell Watson for the launch of his *Encore* album on the Tony Snell show on BBC Radio Merseyside.

And if you're wondering how I got such a perfect Union Jack onto the pie in the picture I'm afraid I can't really take all the credit. I asked Nicky and Tracey Dowson, who own Imaginative Cakes near where I live, to make me a Union Jack in sugar paper to top off my Best of British Pie. When the pie was cooked and still warm I rolled out the Union Jack onto the top of the pastry – great fun!

450 g / 1 lb minced mutton

450 g / 1 lb diced mutton

2 Granny Smith apples, chopped

2 tablespoons brown sugar

Rind of 1 lemon, grated

100 g / 4 oz raisins

½ teaspoon black pepper

½ teaspoon grated nutmeg

½ teaspoon cinnamon

½ teaspoon salt

1 tablespoon cornflour mixed with 300 ml / ½ pint of Guinness

75 ml / 3 fl oz dark rum

450 g / 1 lb shortcrust pastry (see recipe on page 33)

1 egg, beaten, to glaze

SERVES 4–6

Mix the mutton, apples, sugar, grated lemon peel, raisins, spices and seasoning.

Place the ingredients into a deep casserole dish and pour in the beer and the rum.

Roll out the pastry, cover with pastry crust, glaze, and put 3 little cuts in the top of the pastry.

Bake at 170ºC / 325ºF / gas mark 3 for at least 1½ hours until the pie is cooked. Top with union jack sugar paper – or you can even invent your own design!

Rolled loin of mutton (very excellent)

I love old recipes, just read this one from the wonderful Mrs Beeton, it'll make you smile!

About 6lbs of a loin of mutton

½ teaspoonful of pepper

¼ teaspoonful of pounded allspice

¼ teaspoonful of mace

¼ teaspoonful of nutmeg

6 cloves

forcemeat

1 glass of port wine

2 tablespoonfuls of mushroom ketchup

Hang the mutton till tender, bone it, and sprinkle over it pepper, mace, cloves, allspice, and nutmeg in the above proportion, all of which must be pounded into a very fine poweder. Let it remain for a day, then make forcemeat, cover the meat with it, and roll and bind it up firmly. Half bake it in a slow oven, let it grow cold, take off the fat, and put the gravy into a stewpan; flour the meat, put it in the gravy, and stew it till perfectly tender. Now take out the meat, unbind it, add to the gravy wine and ketchup as above, give one boil, and pour over the meat. Serve with red-currant jelly; and, if obtainable, a few mushrooms stewed for a few minutes in the gravy, will be found a great improvement.

Time – 1½ hour to bake the meat, 1½ hour to stew gently.

Average cost, 4s. 9d. Sufficient for 5 or 6 persons.

Seasonable at any time.

This joint will be found very nice if rolled and stuffed, as here directed, and plainly roasted. It should be well basted, and served with a good gravy and currant jelly.

Mrs Beeton's Book of Household Management (1861) (p181).

Small Mutton Pies

Traditionally called Tuppenny Struggles, this pie is a splendid Scottish football terrace warmer. The recipe was given to me by John Fallon, Managing Director of Grant's Haggis, the company which puts haggis into cans rather than sheep's stomachs!

450 g / 1 lb hot water pastry
  (see recipe on page 36)

650 g / 1 lb 6 oz lean mutton,
  minced

Pinch of freshly grated nutmeg

Salt and black pepper

Mutton or lamb stock
  (see recipe on page 49)

1 egg, beaten with milk to glaze

6 small pie tins or muffin
  moulds, lightly buttered

Pre-heat the oven to 200°C / 400°F / gas mark 6.

Prepare the hot water pastry recipe, set aside one third in a warm area for the lids.

Roll out the pastry on a floured surface to 5 mm / ¼ inch thick. Cut out six large circles to fit in the pie tins and six smaller circles for the lids.

Line the tins with the large circles of pastry.

Place the meat into a large bowl; season it well with nutmeg, salt and pepper. Add just enough stock to moisten the meat. Divide the meat equally into the pie tins.

Cover the tops with the remaining circles of pastry and make a small hole in the centre of each pie.

Glaze and place the pies onto a baking sheet.

Bake in the centre of the oven, lowering the heat after 10 minutes to 180°C / 350°F / gas mark 4 for 1 hour.

Ayrshire Lamb with New Potatoes & Wild Mint

I worked in Ayr in the early 1970s at the Pickwick Hotel. My interest then was reading old recipes, which brought out the cookery detective in me. This recipe was in *The Complete Housewife: or accomplished gentlewoman's companion* by E Smith, published in 1739. I have modified the recipe and added some twentieth-century flavours.

25 g / 1 oz beef dripping

1 kg / 2¼ lb lean lamb (Ayrshire if possible), off the bone, diced

900 g / 2 lb new potatoes, washed and diced

150 g / 5 oz diced carrot

225 g / 8 oz sliced onion

1 tablespoon wild mint

25 g / 1 oz plain flour

100 g / 4 oz marrowfat peas

1 teaspoon Worcestershire sauce

300 ml / 10 fl oz lamb stock

Salt and black pepper

1 lb / 450 g shortcrust pastry

1 egg, beaten, to glaze

SERVES 4–6

Pre-heat the oven to 180°C / 350°F / gas mark 4.

In a large saucepan heat the dripping until it is quite hot, add the lamb and very quickly seal and brown it for 3 minutes. Cook slowly for 20 minutes and then add the potatoes, carrot, onion and wild mint, cooking for 2 minutes.

Sprinkle with the flour, stir, then add the peas, Worcestershire sauce and lamb stock and bring to the boil slowly. Remove from the heat, season well and taste. Put the mixture into a 1.2 litre / 2 pint pie dish.

Roll out the pastry and cover the pie dish, sealing and crimping the pastry all around. Trim of any excess pastry and use to decorate, and then glaze.

Bake in the centre of the oven for 50 minutes.

Maimed Hepburn from the croft gate cries,
'Come buy my hot and tottling pies!
Fine mutton pies, fat piping hot,
One for a penny, four for a groat!

Charles Spence, Errol Winter Market.
The Scots Kitchen F Maraian McNeill (1929)

'Posh' Lancashire Hogget Hotpots

This is posh only in the sense that I use the finest ingredients. You will need for this recipe six individual ovenproof pot or pie dishes, 380 ml / ⅔ pint in size. If they don't have lids, cover with double-wrapped, buttered tin foil at the end of the recipe.

2 whole hogget or mutton fillets, trimmed and skinned

30 ml / 2 tablespoons corn oil

Salt and black pepper

250 g / 9 oz button onions, peeled

250 g / 9 oz oyster mushrooms

150 ml / ¼ pint dry white wine

400 ml / 14 fl oz chicken stock

900 g / 2 lb potatoes finely sliced

50 g / 2 oz melted butter

6 rounds buttered tin foil to cover the pots

SERVES 6

Pre-heat the oven 170°C / 325°F / gas mark 3.

Carefully slice the two fillets into 24 discs. Heat the oil in the frying pan and quickly fry and seal them in small batches. Season all the meat and place 4 pieces in each pot.

Brown the onions and divide them between the pots. Repeat the process with the mushrooms.

Mix together the wine and stock and cover the ingredients in each pot with the liquid.

In each pot, arrange the finely sliced potatoes neatly in overlapping circles on top of each other, brushing generously with the melted butter. Season the potatoes lightly.

Put on the pot lids or cover with buttered tin foil and place in the oven for 60 minutes. Remove the foil or lids, raise the temperature to 190°C / 375°F / gas mark 5 and cook for a further 25 minutes until the potatoes are golden brown.

Poultry & game

Sixty years ago chicken was a luxury and most folk ate less than 2½ lbs (1 kilo) of it each year. How things have changed! These days we eat twice that every month, something that has been possible only through battery farming, and the huge suffering this has caused to the birds. Thankfully there has been a massive backlash against this appalling method of rearing chickens, and it is now easy and much more affordable to buy organic, free range or at the very least 'freedom' versions. Yes, this does cost more than the two-for-five-quid shockers, but surely we can all eat a bit less and pay a bit more?

In the case of game, of course, it is by definition free range, since this is defined as any animal hunted for food or not normally domesticated. Although not everyone likes game, its popularity has grown in recent years due to its delicious flavour and low fat content. Game meat has a very different range of flavours from chicken and, perhaps most importantly, is wonderful for helping to create spectacularly tasty pies.

Devonshire Squab (Pigeon) Pie

Not a squab in sight in the original recipe and I feel it should have something similar, so I am making it my way. The Roman cookbook *Apicius* recommended sauces with a combined sweet and sour flavour to accompany roasted or braised squab. In 1607, a monastery recipe book suggested cooking squab with pork fat or bitter limes. There is less information about traditional recipes incorporating squab or pigeon used by commoners, but there is evidence that recipes involving squab were handed down from generation to generation This pie can be found on several pub menus throughout Devon using lamb, beef and chicken rather than pigeon.

450 g / 1 lb Bramley apples, peeled, cored and sliced

2 red onions, peeled and sliced

650 g / 1 lb 6 oz pigeon meat, diced

Salt and black pepper

Pinch of allspice

1 tablespoon brown sugar

150 ml / ¼ pint scrumpy cider

150 ml / ¼ pint chicken stock

300 g / 11 oz shortcrust cheese pastry (see recipe on page 41)

1 egg, beaten, to glaze

SERVES 4–6

Pre-heat the oven to 200°C / 400°F / gas mark 6.

Butter a deep casserole dish and place a layer of apples at the bottom, followed by a layer of sliced onion.

Add half the pigeon meat and season well with salt and pepper and the pinch of allspice.

Repeat the above process, top with brown sugar, pour in the cider and chicken stock. Roll out the pastry and top the pie, crimping the edges and glaze. Cover with cooking foil and place in the centre of the oven for 20 minutes.

Reduce the heat to 170°C / 325°F / gas mark 3, remove the foil and cook for a further 45 minutes.

L.A.'s Chicken, Tarragon & Leek Pie

This is songstress Lily Allen's favourite pie, and she has said she would like to make it on *Celebrity Come Dine with Me*. Well Lily, here's the perfect recipe!

1 whole chicken, deboned and cut into bite size pieces

4 slices cooked ham

4 leeks, chopped

15 ml / 1 tablepsoon freshly chopped tarragon

1 medium onion, chopped

Salt and black pepper

1 pinch ground mace or ground nutmeg

300 ml / ½ pint chicken stock

450 g / 1 lb puff pastry

15 ml / 1 tablespoon milk

125 ml / 4¼ fl oz double cream

SERVES 4–6

Preheat the oven to 180ºC / 350ºF / gas mark 4.

Using a 1.4 litre / 2½ pint baking dish, layer the chicken, ham, leeks, tarragon and onion a couple of times each until the dish is full. Season each layer with a little salt, pepper and mace or nutmeg. Pour the chicken stock over the layers and dampen the edges of the dish.

Roll the pastry out large enough to cover the top of the dish, and place over the top. Crimp the sides down with a fork and trim the excess from the edges. Cut a round hole in the centre of the pastry. Roll the pastry scraps out and cut into strips, using them to form a design, and place lightly over the hole. Brush the entire top with milk and bake for 35 to 45 minutes in the pre-heated oven, until the chicken is cooked through. If the top crust is getting too brown, loosely cover it with greaseproof baking paper or aluminium foil.

While the pie is baking, heat the cream over a low heat. When the pie is cooked, remove from the oven, and carefully remove the design from the hole. Pour the cream into the hole, and replace the design. Let the pie stand for a few minutes before serving.

Chicken & Pigeon Pie

I remember reading a funny letter from an old gentleman in Blackburn when I was writing my *Golden Age of Cookery* book in the early 1980s. I was researching pigeon pies, and this is the recipe he wrote down in his letter, which is shown on the opposite page.

Filling

15 ml / 1 tablespoon cooking oil

25 g / 1 oz butter

450 g / 1 lb pigeon meat

450 g / 1 lb chicken thigh meat

Salt and black pepper

6 slices rindless streaky bacon, finely chopped

8 shallots, peeled and sliced

2 large potatoes, peeled and diced

1 small carrot diced

80 ml / 5 tablespoons brown ale

150 ml / ¼ pint chicken stock

2 tablespoons of double cream

5 tablespoons cranberry jelly

2 tablespoons fresh parsley

Pastry

175 g / 6 oz plain flour

Pinch of salt

110 g / 4 oz butter

1 egg yolk

40 ml cold water, approx

75 g / 3 oz mature Cheddar, grated

SERVES 4–6

Sift the flour with the salt. Rub in the butter until it looks like breadcrumbs. Mix the yolk with the water and grated cheese and then add to the mixture. Mix to a firm dough, chill for 20 minutes and then let it relax for 10 minutes after rolling out.

Pre-heat the oven to 200°C / 400°F / gas mark 6.

Melt the butter with the cooking oil in a large saucepan, add the pigeon and chicken and seal the meat all over, seasoning with salt and pepper. Simmer for 3 minutes then remove the pigeon and chicken meat and place to one side. Put the bacon, shallots, potatoes and carrot in the pan, stirring briskly for a further 3 minutes. Add the ale and chicken stock, bring to the boil and simmer for 25 minutes on a low heat, reducing the stock by at least a third. Return the pigeon and chicken to the pan and allow the sauce to cool slightly, then mix in the double cream and cranberry jelly.

Roll out the pastry to fit a 1.2 litres / 2 pint, pie dish.

Place the mixture in the pie dish, sprinkle with freshly chopped parsley and put on the pastry lid. Wash the top with a little milk and bake in the centre of the oven for 30 minutes.

'If this pie is to be eaten hot, have a nice flaky pastry. If intended cold, shortcrust, preferably, and should be equally rich or nearly so. Grease dish and lay crust round sides and edges. At bottom of dish place slices of cooked potato or any vegetable leftovers, season. Put pie to one side; now cook your pigeons off in stock for ¾ hour in a moderate oven. Let it cool and take all the meat from the bones. Chop it up and put it in a large basin, mix with it, parsley, chopped boiled eggs 2, drop of milk, salt and pepper, drop of gravy to moisten it. Put in pie and put crust on top. Cook in oven until golden brown. After eating – If it's ya dad's pigeons – run like hell!'

We are all familiar with the nursery rhyme about four and twenty blackbirds, which most of us wouldn't take literally. But in actual fact, in medieval times, it was considered highly amusing for live birds to be put inside a large pastry case, from which they would fly out when the pie was cut open at a nobleman's table. It was usually pigeons that were in the joke pie, but blackbirds and other songbirds were considered to be great delicacies and may well have been used too. On a more sensible note, there would normally have been a second pie made which the diners could actually eat!

Lumber-Pye (Venison Pie)

'Let the umbles of a Deer be parboil'd and well clear'd from the Fat; then put to them as Beef-suet as Meat or more and chop all together very fine; To these add three of four pounds of Currans, half a Pound of Sugar, a pint of Sact, a little Rose-water, half a Pound of Candy'd Orange, Lemmon and Citron-peel, Dates stoned and stic'd with Cloves, Mace, Cinnamon, Nutmeg, and a little Salt. Having fill'd your Pye, close it; and when 'tis bak'd, pour in somewhat above half a pint of Canary-Wine.'

from the cookbook The Queen's Closet Opened, 1656

This was the origin of the Christmas mince pie and I actually use this recipe for my mince pies, using minced Sirloin of beef, and when people eat them they always look puzzled and say "I'm sure I can taste meat in your pies!"

Royal Pie (1813)

Another recipe I came across was for a Royal Pie. In 1813, Lord Talbot, then Viceroy of Ireland, presented King George III with 24 woodcock baked in a pie. Since then the custom has been followed of sending one to the reigning sovereign in England every Christmas. In 1929 such a pie was sent by Mr James McNeill, then the Governor-General of the Irish Free State, to HM King George V at Sandringham.

Extra Special Venison Pie for the Christmas Table

Without doubt the key to good pie-making is the pastry. The taste and texture must be right, of course, and the finished pie should look attractive, but definitely not like something from a production line.

900 g / 2 lb rough minced venison

50 g / 2 oz finely chopped onion

150 ml / ¼ pint dry white wine

30 ml / 2 tablespoons brandy

2 ml / ½ teaspoon dried sage

15 ml / 1 tablespoon Dijon mustard

1 Bramley apple, peeled and grated coarsely

Salt and black pepper

Stuffing

175 g / 6 oz packet stuffing (sage and onion)

50 g / 2 oz freshly minced onion

50 g / 2 oz freshly minced Bramley apple

Hot pork or beef stock mixed with 225 g / 8 oz black pudding

2 lb hot water pastry (see recipe on page 36)

1 egg, beaten, to glaze

Pork stock made with a little wine and meat stock

Pre-heat the oven 200C / 400°F / gas mark 6.

Mix the minced venison with the onion, wine, brandy, sage, Dijon mustard, apple and season this well with a generous pinch of salt and some pepper.

Mix the stuffing ingredients in a bowl, using enough of the stock to bind them together.

Line the bottom of each 8–10 cm / 3–4 inch pie mould with hot water pastry.

Quarter fill the lined tin with the meat mixture and then the stuffing mixture, alternating until you have three linings of venison and two of stuffing.

Roll out the remaining pastry, making the lid to fit the pie.

Make a hole in the centre of the pie lid.

Decorate with pastry leaves, egg-glaze and bake for 35 minutes. Reduce the oven to 180C / 350°F / gas mark 4 and continue to bake for a further hour.

Remove the pie from the oven and allow it to cool.

Pour in some pork stock, made up with a little wine and pork stock.

When the jelly has set, wrap the pie in cling film and allow it to mature for two days.

Pheasant & Beefsteak Pie

This was usually served with fresh oysters, so should you wish to be bold add the 12 oysters just before you put the pastry top on.

25 g / 1 oz beef dripping

350 g / 12 oz pheasant meat, cut into chunks

450 g / 1 lb rump steak, cut into chunks

225 g / 8 oz button mushrooms

1 bay leaf

Sprig of thyme

1 teaspoon parsley

10 shallots, peeled and sliced

Salt and black pepper

1 tablespoon plain flour

200 ml / 7 fl oz beef stock

150 ml / 5 fl oz red wine

3 hard-boiled eggs, halved

275 g / 10 oz puff pastry
(see recipe on page 39)

1 egg, beaten, to glaze

SERVES 6

Heat the dripping in a large saucepan and brown the meat, cooking all over for about 4 minutes. Add the mushrooms, bay leaf, thyme, parsley and shallots and cook for a further 3 minutes, seasoning with salt and pepper.

Sprinkle the meat with the flour and cook for 3 minutes, add the beef stock and red wine and simmer gently for 1 hour.

Carefully discard the bay leaf and thyme. With a slotted spoon remove the meat and mushrooms from the saucepan and place into a deep pie dish.

Reduce the stock left in the saucepan by half. Meanwhile pre-heat the oven 180ºC / 350ºF / gas mark 4 and roll out the puff pastry to fit the pie dish.

Pour the beef stock onto the meat, then place the egg halves on top and cover with the pastry, generously glaze the top of the pastry and bake in the centre of the oven for 40 minutes.

The cost per portion of this pie worked out at 1s 3d in 1900

Florence White

Florence White was born in 1863 in Peckham, London, and before the age of eight she had lost her mother and been blinded in one eye. This latter tragedy is said to have ruined her prospects for marriage, and she embarked on a career which included governess, teacher, lady's companion and cook/housekeeper. She was also a writer for *The Lady* and *Home Chat* magazines and she later became the first journalist to specialise in cookery, paving the way for a plethora of subsequent cookery writers. Her particular interest was traditional English cookery, which she believed was the best in the world but in danger of being lost unless recipes were saved and published for future generations. She wrote *Good Things in England* in 1932 and it proved to be as great an influence on the culinary world as had the work of Mrs Beeton before her, and Elizabeth David many years later.

In 1928 she established the English Folk Cookery Association, which recorded hundreds of recipes, had an 'experiment kitchen' to update and if necessary improve some of the recipes, and also held events to promote and celebrate what they found. The association also published a directory of restaurants and cafes offering good English cooking, entitled the *Good Food Register*, and which Florence edited in later years. She died in 1940, and her last book, *Good English Food* was published posthumously in 1952. It was to be another 50 years, however, before the food of the British Isles was once more being widely championed. She would no doubt have loved to have been a food writer now, in the twenty-first century, when her enthusiasms and ideas are once again in the ascendant.

A Sixteenth-century Shropshire Pie

This recipe is supplied by a Shropshire lady who gives its date as 1778 and is taken from *Good Things in England* by Florence White.

There are several unusual recipes in Florence's cookbook, such as a seventeenth-century Rook Pie which is cooked with beef steak in a flaky pastry crust (this would have been as tough as an old boot!), and a Mock Pork Pie using egg and bacon.

In the Shropshire Pie were 2 rabbits, jointed, with their livers made into savoury balls, pork fat, oysters and artichoke bottoms with red wine. Far too rich for today's tastes, but I would loved to have lived through that era.

Nineteenth-century Poachers' Pie or Rabbit in a Crust

Rabbits are very slowly disappearing from today's menus and it really is a loss. The flavour and texture of rabbit meat is something that you really cannot describe until you have eaten it, and for this recipe you can't really substitute with any other meat than hare.

In Sussex, rabbits are always cooked in cider, and this recipe contains a little flavour of that county. In Durham they add boiled bacon and serve it with a cream sauce for a supper dish.

350 g / 12 oz shortcrust pastry

450 g / 1 lb boneless rabbit, skinned and cubed

100 g / 4 oz York ham, diced

1 carrot, peeled and finely diced

350 g / 12 oz sliced potatoes

1 large apple, peeled, cored and diced

12 button onions, peeled

100 g / 4 oz button mushrooms

Salt and black pepper

1 tablespoon freshly chopped parsley

A generous pinch of rosemary and thyme

150 ml / ¼ pint strong dry cider

300 ml / ½ pint chicken stock

1 large tablespoon cornflour, blended with a little cider

1 egg, beaten, to glaze

SERVES 4–6

Pre-heat the oven 220°C / 425°F / gas mark 7.

Fill a large casserole dish 1.75 litre / 3 pints with alternative layers of rabbit, ham, carrot, potatoes, onions, apple and mushrooms, seasoning each layer with salt, pepper and the herbs.

Fill the casserole with the stock, cover and bake in the centre of the oven for approx 30 minutes and then thicken the stock with the cornflour.

Roll out the pastry and place the pastry lid onto the casserole and trim the edge, sealing the pie all round, make a small hole in the centre of the pastry to allow the steam to come through and glaze.

Bake in the centre of the oven for 1 hour at 180°C/ 350°F / gas mark 4.

Serve this with crusty bread and a glass of Sussex mead

Twenty-first Century Rabbit Pie, or 'The Credit Munch'!

I have made this pie many, many times and I am always being asked for it. I originally created it for Granada television for a series with my old buddy Fred Talbot entitled the Credit Munch, for which I made several pie recipes.

25 g / 1 oz beef dripping

675 g / 1½ lb roughly chopped rabbit meat, bones removed

250 g / ½ lb naturally cured rindless back bacon, diced

450 g / 1 lb potatoes, peeled and diced

150 g / 5 oz diced carrot

100 g / 4 oz garden peas

2 large onions, peeled and sliced

1 tablespoon mixed herbs

25 g / 1 oz plain flour

300 ml / ½ pint chicken stock

50 ml / 3 tablespoons port

Salt and white pepper

225 g / 8 oz black pudding, skin removed and diced

2 lb My mum and gran's suet pastry (see recipe on page 35)

SERVES 6–8

Pre-heat the oven to 200°C / 400°F / gas mark 6.

In a large saucepan heat the dripping until it is quite hot and add the rabbit and bacon. Quickly seal and brown the meat for 5 minutes, then add the potatoes, carrot, peas, onions and mixed herbs, cooking for 4 minutes. Sprinkle with the flour, stir, add the stock and port, bring to the boil and simmer for 25 minutes, seasoning with salt and pepper. Put the mixture into a 1.2 litre / 2 pint pie dish, scattering the diced black pudding over the top (this helps to thicken the pie during the cooking process).

Roll the pastry as for game pie (see page 120), cover the pie dish, sealing and crimping the pastry all round. Trim off any excess and use to decorate. Brush with milk and bake in the centre of the oven for 45 minutes.

Aylesbury Game Pie

These days it is not difficult to buy a range of game meats from butchers, markets and supermarkets, and often both fresh and frozen options are available.

Traditionally, game pie should be made with a puff pastry crust but I am going to use my own suet crust pastry, which I created especially for this recipe.

50 g / 2 oz butter

50 g / 2 oz dripping or lard

700 g / 1½ lb of mixed game meat consisting of one third each of haunch of venison, rabbit and pheasant, using pure meat with no gristle and all fat removed

225 g / 8 oz button mushrooms

225 g / 8 oz shallots, peeled

2 cloves garlic

3 tablespoons plain flour seasoned with salt and pepper

300 ml / 10 fl oz claret

300 ml / 10 fl oz good beef stock

1 onion, chopped

8 juniper berries

Pinch of allspice and marjoram

1 teaspoon salt

Black pepper

1 lb game suet pastry (see recipe on page 36)

SERVES 6–8

Put the fats into a very large saucepan and heat gently. Add the game meat and seal by cooking it for 5 minutes, extracting the juices and browning the meat quickly.

Add the mushrooms, shallots and garlic, cooking for a further 4 minutes. Sprinkle with the flour and cook for 3 minutes, then slowly add the claret and beef stock. Add the rest of the ingredients, take the pan from the heat and allow to stand for 6 hours.

Bring the game mix to the boil and simmer, reducing the stock by half, cooking for at least 25 minutes. Place the game and the sauce into a 1.1 litre / 2 pint pie dish.

Roll out the pastry and cover the pie dish, sealing all round edges. Glaze with a little milk and bake in the centre of the oven for 50 minutes at 180°C / 350°F / gas mark 4.

A Famous Grouse Within a Grouse Pie

In Scotland grouse pie is always served with fried bread and rowan jelly, so I have combined these ingredients into this wonderfully traditional grouse pie, using Famous Grouse whisky for the flavour.

15 ml / 1 tablespoon cooking oil

25 g / 1 oz butter

450 g / 1 lb grouse meat

Salt and black pepper

6 slices rindless streaky bacon, finely chopped

8 shallots, peeled and sliced

1 small carrot diced

75 ml / 3 fl oz Famous Grouse whisky

150 ml / 5 fl oz chicken stock

2 tablespoons of double cream

5 tablespoons rowan jelly

275 g / 10 oz puff pastry (see recipe on page 39)

2 tablespoons fresh parsley

2 slices of white bread, cut into quarters

25 g / 1 oz beef dripping and 25 g / 1 oz butter

SERVES 4–6

Pre-heat the oven to 200°C / 400°F / gas mark 6.

Melt the butter with the cooking oil in a large saucepan, add the grouse meat and seal the meat all over. Season with salt and pepper, simmering for 3 minutes, then add the bacon, shallots and carrot, stirring briskly for a further 3 minutes. Add the whisky and chicken stock, bring to the boil and simmer for 25 minutes on a low heat, reducing the stock by at least a third.

Allow the grouse and sauce to cool slightly and blend in the double cream and rowan jelly.

Roll out the pastry to fit a 1.2 litre / 2 pint pie dish.

Put the game mixture into the pie dish, sprinkle with freshly chopped parsley, and then top with rolled out puff pastry lid. Wash the top with a little milk and bake in the centre of the oven for 25 minutes.

Fry the bread in the dripping and butter and place around the pie when it is ready to be served.

Traditional Game Pie

Today you can buy the complete mix of game meat from your butcher or from some supermarkets. They stock it fresh and frozen, and is not difficult at all to purchase.

Although game pie is traditionally made with puff pastry I like to use my shortcrust pastry instead, using leftover bits for decoration.

50 g / 2 oz butter

50 g / 2 oz dripping or lard

775 g / 1½ lb of mixed game meat consisting of one third each of haunch of venison, rabbit and pheasant, using pure meat with no gristle and all fat removed

225 g / 8 oz wild or oyster mushrooms

225 g / 8 oz shallots, peeled

2 cloves garlic

3 tablespoons seasoned plain flour

300 ml / 10 fl oz claret

300 ml / 10 fl oz good beef stock

1 onion chopped

8 juniper berries

Pinch of allspice and marjoram

1 teaspoon salt

Black pepper

2 lb shortcrust pastry (see recipe on page 33)

SERVES 6–8

In a very large saucepan heat the fats gently. Add the game meat and seal it by cooking for 5 minutes, extracting the juices and browning the meat quickly.

Add the chopped mushroom, shallots and garlic, cooking for a further 4 minutes. Sprinkle with the flour and cook for 3 minutes, then slowly add the claret and beef stock. Add the rest of the ingredients. Take the pan from the heat and allow to stand for 6 hours.

Make up the pastry and let it rest.

Bring the game mix to the boil and simmer, reducing the stock by half, cooking for at least 25 minutes. Place the game and the sauce into a 1.2 litre / 2 pint pie dish.

Roll out the pastry and cover the pie dish, sealing the edges all round, making decorative leaves with any leftover pastry. Coat with a little milk and bake in the centre of the oven for 50 minutes at 180°C / 350°F / gas mark 4.

Kitchiner's **Pigeon** or **Lark** pie

Dr William Kitchiner (1775–1827) was an optician, musician, inventor of telescopes and brilliant cook who wrote *The Housekeeper's Oracle* in 1817. The book was a bestseller and Kitchiner a real English eccentric, who travelled with a portable taste cabinet which housed his unique spices and sauces, and who made and cleaned up after all his recipes himself! I love *The Cook's Oracle* and that its author was such a character, so much so that I and Colin Cooper English wrote *Dr William Kitchiner: Regency Eccentric* (we were really proud that the book came second for the André Simon Award in 1993).

The bird's feet were often added to show what was in the pie, and another recipe of the period suggests that the feet should be left poking through a hole in the pastry, just to make it absolutely clear! To make this pie use my recipe for Pheasant and Beefsteak Pie (see page 114), and replace the pheasant with pigeon.

Truss half a dozen fine large Pigeons as for stewing, season them with Pepper and Salt: lay at the bottom of the dish a Rump Steak of about a pound weight, cut into pieces and trimmed neatly, seasoned and beat out with a chopper: on it lay the pigeons, the yolks of three Eggs boiled hard, and a gill of broth or water, and over these a layer of steaks. Wet the edge of the dish, and cover it over with Puff-paste, or the paste as directed for seasoned pies. Wash it over with Yolk of Egg, and ornament it with leaves of paste, and the feet of the Pigeons; bake it an hour and a half in a moderate heated oven: before it is sent to table make an aperture in the top, and pour in some good Gravy quite hot.

Cheesy eggy stuff!

I adore cheese, as you might already know, and I've had huge fun over the years creating recipes that include all sorts of varieties. I love the flavours in my Four Layer Cheese Pie, and my Gorgeous Cheddar Cheese Pie, but there are lots more ideas in this chapter that really do make the most of both cheese and eggs – and of course you can always experiment with your own particular favourites.

Talking of eggs, I'm afraid I've got to step up onto my soap box again – only briefly, but I'm sure you can see what's coming! You guessed it: all the eggs I use are free range, and really these days I think everyone can afford them; they have certainly come down in price hugely in the last decade or so. Organic is even better, of course, but they do cost a little more usually, although in my opinion it is worth it.

A Gorgeous Cheddar Cheese Pie

I am using three different cheeses from Cheddar for this tasty pie, with a lining of spinach and apples between each layer. If you can't get hold of the Cheddar Gorge Cheese Company's cheeses (see page 135) just use similar top quality varieties, including a blue and a mature. I would serve this cold with an ice-cold glass of Somerset cider, but it would work hot too.

600 g / 1 lb 5 oz shortcrust pastry

50 g / 2 oz butter

450 g / 1 lb onions, thinly sliced

250 g / 9 oz spinach leaf, blanched and chopped

Salt and black pepper

225 g / 8 oz each of grated:
Natural Blue Cheddar, Cave Matured Cheddar and Fosse Way Fleece Ewes Milk Cheese

3 eggs

150 ml / ¼ pint full fat milk

100 ml / 6 tablespoons of double cream

100 ml / 6 tablespoons of apple sauce

2 apples, cored and peeled, thinly sliced

100 ml / 6 tablespoons of crab apple jelly

1 teaspoon Worcestershire sauce

1 egg yolk mixed with 2 tablespoons of milk, to glaze

SERVES 4–6

Pre-heat the oven to 190°C / 375°F / gas mark 5.

Roll out the pastry and use two-thirds to line a deep 25 cm / 10 inch ring pie tin or loose-based cake tin, greased with a little butter.

Fry the onions in half the butter for 3 minutes. Add the spinach and cook for 2 minutes, season well with pepper and a little salt. Let the mixture cool.

Into three separate bowls grate each cheese, adding an egg, 50 ml / 3 tablespoons milk and 2 tablespoons cream to each bowl, together with pepper and a little Worcestershire sauce. Mix thoroughly.

Lay a lining of apple, followed by the spinach and onion mixture onto the base of the pie, and then top with the Natural Blue Cheddar mix and apple sauce.

Add another layer of spinach and onion and top with the Cave Matured Cheddar mix and crab apple jelly.

Follow with a final layer of spinach and onion topped with a last layer of the Fleece Ewes Milk mix.

Top with the last of the apple and use the remaining pastry to make the lid, sealing the edges and decorating the top with any leftover pastry trimmings and then glaze.

Bake in the centre of the oven for 60 minutes until golden brown.

Allow the pie to cool completely and then chill it for at least 2 hours. Slice and serve with a vine tomato salad.

Tracy & Mike's Spanish Cheese Pie

One of my closest friends is my old school pal Phil Berry, whose daughter Tracy lives in Spain with her family. She brought me some Garcia Baquero cheese, made from goat's and sheep's milk, and I grated it, added some cream and 2 egg yolks, seasoned with ground black pepper, and cooked it slowly, like you would when making a Welsh rarebit. It was so good, I thought what a fantastic cheese pie it would make, and here's the recipe I came up with. I was supposed to be having a break from cooking, but when it comes to pies I just can't help myself!

450 g / 1 lb shortcrust pastry
    (see recipe on page 33)

25 g / 1 oz butter

1 leek finely chopped

200 g / 7 oz mild goat's cheese

200 g / 7 oz sheep's cheese

100 g / 4 oz potatoes, cooked
    and diced

100 g / 4 oz Cox's Orange
    Pippin, diced

2 egg yolks

75 ml / 3 fl oz cream

Pinch smoked cayenne pepper

White pepper

1 egg, beaten, to glaze

SERVES 4–6

Pre-heat the oven to 220ºC / 425ºF / gas mark 7.

Roll out the pastry on a floured surface, dividing into two thirds for the base and one third for the lid.

Grease and line a pie dish with the pastry.

Melt the butter in a saucepan and gently fry the leek until it is transparent, about 4 minutes, and allow to cool. Put it with the cheese and the rest of the ingredients into a large bowl and mix thoroughly.

Place the mixture into the lined pie dish and top with the remaining pastry and glaze.

Bake in the oven for 30 minutes until golden brown.

Four Layer Cheese Party Pie

The Bridges are a cheese-loving family (apart from my mum!), and we all enjoy the full-fat versions most, my favourite being Stilton, with grapes and a glass of vintage port. But for something completely different you must try the pie I always bake whenever I have cheese left over from the cheese board.

The taste and look of this Four Layer Cheese Pie, which I created for Wigan Food Festival in 2009 with Kat Pickett, really are exceptional because of the quality and hues of the cheeses used. The four colours of cheeses, with a lining of spinach, fruit and onion between each layer, give a fantastic marble effect when you slice into the pie. My suggestions are Red Leicester, Lancashire, Sage Derby and Blue Wensleydale or Stilton, in that order, for colour perfection, but you can use your own favourites as long as they are of different colours. This is ideal for a lunch served warm with a tomato and beetroot salad.

700 g / 1½ lb shortcrust pastry
(see recipe on page 33)

50 g / 2 oz butter

450 g / 1 lb red onions,
chopped

350 g / 12 oz spinach leaf,
trimmed, blanched and
chopped

Salt and black pepper

2 apples, cored and peeled,
thinly sliced

225 g / 8 oz each of the
following grated cheeses:
Red Leicester, Lancashire,
Sage Derby and Blue
Wensleydale or Stilton

120 ml / 8 tablespoons of apple
sauce

120 ml / 8 tablespoons of
gooseberry puree or jam

120 ml / 8 tablespoons of
cranberry sauce

1 teaspoon of freshly grated
nutmeg

3 teaspoons Worcestershire
sauce

1 egg, beaten with 1
tablespoon of milk, to glaze

SERVES 8–10.

Pre-heat the oven to 190°C / 375°F / gas mark 5.

Roll out the pastry and use two-thirds to line a deep 25 cm / 10 inch ring pie tin, or loose-based cake tin, greased with a little butter.

Fry the onion in half the butter for 3 minutes. Add the spinach and cook for 2 minutes, season well with pepper and a little salt.

Lay a lining of apple and the spinach and onion on the base of the pie, and then cover with the Red Leicester and apple sauce.

Add another layer of spinach and onion with the Sage Derby and gooseberry puree or jam.

The next spinach and onion layer is topped with Lancashire, and you repeat the process with the final cheese, Blue Wensleydale or Stilton, and the cranberry sauce, adding a sprinkle of grated nutmeg and the Worcestershire sauce.

Finally, top with the remaining apple and put the pastry lid on the pie, sealing the edges, decorating the top with any leftover pastry, and glazing.

Bake in the centre of the oven for 60 minutes until golden brown. Allow to cool for at least 20 minutes and serve at room temperature with the salad and a glass of chilled dry cider.

Lancashire Family Cheese & Onion

You can create lots of variations of this pie: for example, add leeks for Likky Pie (see page 77), or grilled streaky bacon for a bacon and cheese pie, etc. The basis of every pie, of course, is to season the filling well before putting the lid on!

450 g / 1 lb shortcrust or puff pastry (see recipes on pages 33 and 39)

25 g / 1 oz butter

1 large onion, peeled and chopped

275 g / 10 oz creamy Lancashire cheese, grated

100 g / 4 oz potatoes, cooked and diced

2 eggs, beaten with a little cream

Pinch cayenne pepper

Salt

1 egg, beaten, to glaze

SERVES 4–6

Pre-heat the oven to 220ºC / 425ºF / gas mark 7.

Roll out the pastry on to a floured surface, using two thirds for the base and the rest for the topping.

Grease and line a pie dish with the pastry.

Melt the butter in a saucepan and gently fry the onion until it is transparent, about 4 minutes, and allow it to cool. Put it with the cheese and the rest of the ingredients into a large bowl and mix thoroughly.

Place the mixture into the lined pie dish and top with the remaining pastry and glaze.

Bake in the oven for 30 minutes until golden brown.

For extra flavour add a little sliced apple or leeks

Marco Polo's Pie

This is a recipe I created for my *Golden Age of Cookery* book in the eighties and it's great for barbecues served with a well-seasoned, medium rare steak or tuna. This pie is named in honour of the great explorer because it uses pasta, that most Italian of ingredients.

25 g butter

1 onion, peeled and chopped

1 carrot finely diced

200 g / 7 oz wild mushrooms

350 g / 12 oz shortcrust pastry (see recipe on page 33)

1 egg, beaten, to glaze

225 g / 8 oz cooked macaroni

200 g / 7 oz cooked spinach

115 g / 4½ oz grated Cheddar cheese

350 g / 12 oz vine tomatoes, peeled, deseeded and chopped

4 eggs

150 ml / ½ pint double cream

150 ml / ½ pint full fat milk

½ teaspoon dried thyme

Salt and black pepper

SERVES 4–6

Pre-heat the oven to 180ºC / 350ºF / gas mark 4.

Melt the butter in a saucepan and fry off the onion and carrot for 5 minutes, adding the mushrooms and cooking for a further 4 minutes. Allow them to cool.

Line a tin with pastry and blind bake for 15 minutes. Seal the cooked pastry with egg glaze and bake for a further minute.

Whisk together the eggs, cream and milk and then add the mushroom mixture with the rest of the ingredients.

Pour the mixture into the pie case and bake for 35 minutes until set. Allow to cool and slice.

Picnic Pie

What a pie! This truly is an eighteenth-century masterpiece if you can keep the yolks whole. Using layers of York ham, raw eggs, and cheese, this was the forerunner of the ever-popular ham and egg pie.

350 g / 12 oz shortcrust pastry
  (see recipe on page 33)

450 g / 1 lb York ham, thinly
  sliced

12 whole raw eggs

225 g / 8 oz grated Cheddar
  cheese

Salt and black pepper

1 egg, beaten with a
  little milk, to glaze

SERVES 6

Pre-heat the oven to 190°C / 375°F / gas mark 5.

Roll out two-thirds of the pastry and grease and line a deep pie dish.

Layer the slices of ham, whole raw eggs (trying not to burst the yolks) and cheese, seasoning each layer with salt and pepper, and ending with a layer of ham.

Cover the pie with a pastry lid, seal and glaze.

Bake in the oven for 25 minutes. Let it rest until just warm and serve with wholemeal bread and butter.

All Day Breakfast Pie

This pie is always being requested by friends and family and makes an ideal lunch snack. I came up with the idea on the Big Breakfast Show with Chris Evans, when I had huge quantities of bacon, sausage, black pudding and eggs which I decided could be used to make a mega pie for all the programme folk later in the day. They loved it, and a breakfast pie was born!

275 g / 10 oz cheese pastry
(see recipe on page 41)

225 g / 8 oz grilled crispy back
bacon, chopped

225 g / 8 oz cooked Cumberland
sausage, sliced

6 eggs, whisked

1 large King Edward potato,
cooked, peeled and diced

1 black pudding diced

2 tablespoons of double cream

2 tablespoons fresh parsley

Salt and black pepper

1 egg, beaten with a little
milk, to glaze

Pre-heat the oven to 200ºC / 400ºF / gas mark 6.

Lightly grease a 20 cm / 8 inch non-stick pie tin and roll out the cheese pastry to line it, keeping enough for the top.

Place all the ingredients into a large bowl and mix them thoroughly, season with salt and pepper.

Place the mixture into the lined pie tin, sprinkle with freshly chopped parsley and put on the pastry lid and glaze.

Bake in the centre of the oven for 35 minutes.

You can add some baked beans to the pie should you wish to

Lancashire Tart

I first tasted this fantastic tart at Kevin Berkin's Fence Gate Inn near Burnley. Kevin is famous in Lancashire for his homemade sausages, and his chef made this for me, so I asked if I could reproduce the recipe and here is the result. This is so tasty and you can make it your own by using your local bacon and cheese.

350 g / 12 oz shortcrust pastry (see recipe on page 33)

1 egg, beaten, to glaze

200 g / 7 oz real Lancashire black pudding, skin removed

200 g / 7 oz pork or Cumberland sausage meat

150 g / 5 oz slices of naturally cured smoked bacon, trimmed

2 large potatoes peeled and cut into 3 mm slices

250 ml / 8 fl oz full fat milk

150 ml / ½ pint double cream

5 eggs

Salt and black pepper

500 g / 1 lb 2 oz grated Lancashire cheese

Chopped parsley

SERVES 14 PORTIONS AS STARTER
OR 8 AS A MAIN COURSE

Pre-heat the oven to 180°C / 350°F / gas mark 4.

Line the tart case with shortcrust pastry and blind bake for 15–20 minutes.

Reduce the oven to 140°C / 275°F / gas mark 1.

Seal the cooked pastry with the glaze and bake for a further minute.

Make the black pudding into a round pâté, cover with cling film and flatten out to fit the tart case. Repeat this process with the sausage meat. Grill the bacon until crisp and then chop into fine pieces and allow to cool. Trim any fat from the bacon.

Steam the sliced potatoes until just partly cooked (if a steamer is not available simply boil).

Mix together the milk, cream and egg, seasoning slightly.

To assemble the tart, start with the layer of black pudding, then a layer of potato in the bottom of the tart then a ladle of cream mixture, a sprinkle of Lancashire cheese and a pinch of parsley (look at the picture for guidance!).

This process is repeated with the sausage layer next, then bacon, ending with sliced potato, and finally sprinkling chopped parsley and Lancashire cheese on top.

Bake for 40 minutes at 140°C / 275°F / gas mark 1 until the liquid is set. When cooling, place a plate with a weight on top of the tart to compress the layers.

A Lancashire tart with layers of traditional British pork or Cumberland sausage meat, black pudding, smoked bacon and scallop potatoes, topped with Lancashire cheese and accompanied by a herb salad and a spicy tomato dressing.

Yorkshire Egg & Bacon Flan

I remember having this with a fresh asparagus salad at the Angel at Hetton, near Skipton, nearly 20 years ago, when the late and very wise Denis Watkins would tell you 'this is not a quiche but a flan – you must remember that bacon was once the only meat that a Yorkshire farmer could afford and so began a love affair'. How right he was! When you think about it, the Scotch egg uses the same main ingredients for a quick farmer's lunch, because it makes sense. The pastry recipe was taught to me by my mother when I was about 15 years old and I have been using it ever since. Any leftover pastry you can bag up and freeze to be used whenever you want flan or a quiche pastry.

Pastry

350 g / 12 oz plain flour
Pinch of salt
75 g / 3 oz lard
75 g / 3 oz butter
100 ml 4 fl oz cold water, approx
1 egg, beaten with a little milk, to glaze

Filling

175 g / 6 oz naturally cured bacon, rind removed, cut into 5 cm / 2 inch strips
3 eggs, plus one extra egg yolk
150 ml / ¼ pint single cream
Salt and white pepper

SERVES 4–6

Pre-heat oven 170ºC / 350ºF / gas mark 3 with a baking sheet in.

Sift the flour with the salt. Rub in the lard and butter until it looks like breadcrumbs.

Add just enough water and mix to a firm dough.

Let the pastry relax for 30 minutes after rolling out.

Line a lightly greased 30 cm / 12 inch flan tin, ensuring that there is no overlapping pastry, press very firmly on the base and sides of the pastry and prick it all over with a fork. Blind bake for 12 minutes and then brush the base all over with the glaze, return to the oven for a further 5 minutes.

Your case is now ready for the filling.

Re-set the oven to 190ºC / 375ºF / gas mark 5.

Quickly fry the bacon strips for 5 minutes and allow them to cool.

Mix all the ingredients together and pour the mixture into the flan case.

Bake the flan in the centre of the oven for 30 minutes.

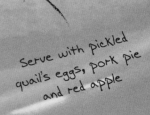

Serve with pickled quail's eggs, pork pie and red apple

In praise of British Cheddar

Funnily enough, versions of this quintessentially British cheese are made all over the world, but it was originally made only in the English village of Cheddar, in Somerset. The cheese is 'Cheddared' to give it its characteristic taste and texture, which involves chopping, turning and pressing the curds to squeeze the whey out, making the cheese drier and harder. It is the most popular cheese in Britain, selling almost a billion pounds worth each year, which is more than half of the entire UK cheese market, and I reckon we'd all be lost without it!

The land around the village of Cheddar has been at the centre of England's dairy industry since at least the fifteenth century, with the earliest references to Cheddar cheese dating from 1170. Now, more than 700 years later, the only company still making the cheese in the village is the Cheddar Gorge Cheese Company, a small producer of entirely handmade cheeses. Just over 3 years ago they started to mature some of their Cheddar in the world-renowned caves, and the added flavour won gold for their Cave Matured Cheddar at the British Cheese Awards. I do like to see a little fish, rather than one of the big boys, winning awards, and, as the owners say, 'it does seem fitting that the best Cheddar has returned to its birthplace.'

To order the cheese and find out more about the company, visit www.cheddargorgecheeseco.co.uk.

Scott of the Antarctic took 3500 lbs of Cheddar, made in Cheddar, on his polar expedition in 1901

It took the milk of 700 cows to make a huge drum of Cheddar for Queen Victoria, and it weighed over 1200 lbs!

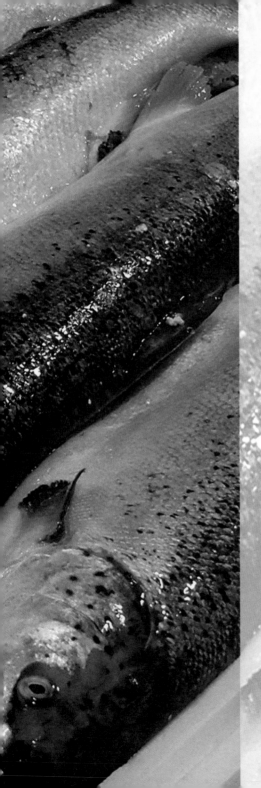

Fish & seafood pies

Fish was once a very important staple for families throughout Great Britain, and each coastal area had their own fish or seafood pie. An eel pie recipe from Richmond in 1873 includes the bone and skins of two Thames eels, but this, along with many seventeenth- and eighteenth-century recipes I have in books I own, would not really suit modern tastes. It is fun, though, to look at the recipes, so look out for some of the ones I have chosen.

Stargazy Pie

I reckon this fishy section must start with Stargazy Pie, a very famous, slightly mad, Cornish dish. The fish used in the traditional recipe are pilchards, which were plentiful in Cornwall and were often hung on lines to dry, or were pickled.

There is a lovely legend behind the pie which tells of a prolonged period of stormy weather in the nineteenth century, which for many days and nights prevented the fishermen of the tiny south Cornwall village of Mousehole from taking their boats out. The villagers were said to be on the brink of starvation when a brave old widower, Tom Bawcock, risked his life to take his vessel into the raging sea, miraculously coming back with a huge catch. A giant pie, big enough to feed all the people of Mousehole, was baked in celebration, with the heads of the fish left on, poking out of the pastry lid and looking towards the heavens – presumably giving thanks to God for saving the people of the village. There are other stories, and variations on this one, but whatever the true origins of the pie, the cookery detective in me is here to tell you that although leaving the heads might not be to everyone's taste, it is actually a jolly good thing! Some of the beneficial omega 3 oils are definitely lost if the heads are removed, so leaving them on really maximises the goodness.

My version, which I created for pie manufacturers, using fresh fillets and with a filling that includes free range boiled eggs and bacon, is like a Cornish all-in-one breakfast pie. The piemakers never did market the idea, though, despite the fact that there wasn't a fish head in sight!

6 to 8 pilchards or herring fillets, bone and skin removed

50 g / 2 oz butter

25 g / 1 oz flour

150 g / 5 fl oz warm milk

150 g / 5 fl oz cider

1 tablespoon sherry

1 teaspoon anchovy essence

75 g / 3 oz Cheddar cheese, grated

2 hard boiled eggs, chopped

175 g / 6 oz streaky bacon, rindless, grilled and chopped

225 g / 8 oz shortcrust pastry (see recipe on page 33)

1 egg, beaten, to glaze

SERVES 4–6

Pre-heat the oven to 200°C / 400°F / gas mark 6.

Put the fish into a large saucepan and fry them gently in the butter for 4 minutes on either side, then carefully place them into the bottom of a pie dish.

Add the flour to the butter in the frying pan and cook for 1 minute, slowly blend in the warm milk and cider to make a smooth sauce, then add the sherry and anchovy essence, cooking for a further 2 minutes, stirring constantly.

Cover the herring fillets with the cheese, boiled egg, and bacon. Pour over just enough of the sauce to cover the fish.

Roll out the pastry, cover the pie dish, and glaze.

Bake in the centre of the oven for 30 minutes.

Rabbit & Crayfish Stargazy Pie

This is the creation of the *Great British Menu*'s Mark Hix, and he has kindly given me his permission to use his recipe. I think it is a wonderful play on a classic recipe.

Front and back and legs from 4 wild rabbits

Salt and black pepper

3 tablespoons plain flour, plus extra for dusting

2–3 tablespoons vegetable oil

2 onions, finely chopped

Large knob unsalted butter

150 ml / 5 fl oz English dry cider

2 litres / 3½ pints hot chicken stock

500 g / 1 lb 2 oz good quality puff pastry made with butter (see recipe on page 39 for guidance)

1 egg, beaten, to glaze

For the crayfish

1 teaspoon fennel seeds

12 black peppercorns

Few sprigs of thyme

2 star anise

1 bay leaf

1 tablespoon salt

24 live freshwater crayfish

1 litre / 1¾ pints chicken stock

SERVES 4–6

Season the rabbit legs with salt and pepper, and dust them with one tablespoon of the flour. Heat the oil in a heavy frying pan until hot, and then lightly brown the rabbit over a medium heat for 3–4 minutes on each side. Carefully remove and drain on kitchen paper.

In a large lidded saucepan, gently fry the onions in the butter for 2–3 minutes until softened, but not coloured. Dust with the remaining flour and stir well over a low heat for a minute, then gradually add the cider and the hot stock, stirring to prevent lumps from forming. Bring to the boil.

Add the rabbit legs and season lightly with more salt and pepper. Cover with the lid. Simmer gently for about one hour or until the rabbit is tender. Remove the rabbit legs and leave to cool. The sauce should be fairly thick – if it's not, continue simmering until it has reduced by half.

For the crayfish, bring a large saucepan of water to the boil with the fennel seeds, peppercorns, thyme, star anise, bay leaf and salt. Simmer for five minutes. Plunge the crayfish into the liquid, bring the water quickly back to the boil and simmer for 1½ minutes. Drain and leave to cool.

Pick out four similar-sized crayfish for the garnish and set aside. Peel the rest, including the large claws, first removing the head and then squeezing the shell between thumb and forefinger to crack it. Set the meat aside. Crush the shells a little, put them in a saucepan with the chicken stock and simmer for 30 minutes. Strain the stock through a sieve into a clean pan and boil to reduce to 4–5 tablespoons. Mix the reduced stock into the rabbit sauce.

Once the rabbit legs are cool, remove the meat from the bones. Mix the rabbit meat into the sauce with the crayfish meat. Turn the mixture into a large pie dish or four individual dishes.

Pre-heat the oven to 200°C / 400°F / gas mark 6.

Roll out the pastry on a floured surface until about 3 mm / ⅛ inch thick. Using a sharp knife cut out a lid that is about 2 cm / ¾ inch larger all round than the top of the pie dish. (Or, if you are using individual dishes, cut the pastry into quarters, roll out and cut out four lids.) Brush the edge of the pastry lid with a little beaten egg, and then lay it on top of the dish, egg-washed side against the rim. Trim the edge and press down to seal. Cut four small slits in the pastry lid (or a small slit in the centre of each of the individual ones) and insert the whole crayfish, keeping the top half of the body above the pastry lid. Brush the pastry with more beaten egg.

Bake the pie for 30–35 minutes or until the pastry is golden brown (small pies will take about 25 minutes); cover the crayfish with foil if they start to brown.

Serve with greens or mashed root vegetables such as celeriac or parsnip and / or small boiled potatoes with chopped herbs.

Salmon Pie, 1823

Make some puff pastry

Clean and scale a middling piece of salmon

Cut it into 3 or 4 pieces according to the size of your dish

Season it pretty high with mace, cloves, pepper and salt

Put some butter at the bottom, and lay in the salmon

Take the meat of a lobster cut small and pound it with some anchovy

Melt as much butter as you think proper, stir the lobster and anchovy into it with a glass of white wine and a little nutmeg

Pour this over the salmon, lay on the top crust, and let it be well baked

Flaky Organic Scottish Salmon Pie

In Scotland we use fresh salmon or Finnan haddock, in Cornwall haddock with some white crab meat, and northern folk are cod lovers. With this pie you can choose, and you can add some prawns too if you wish, and top with potato instead of pastry.

450 g / 1 lb fresh organic
    salmon, boned and skinned

600 ml / 1 pint of milk

25 g / 1 oz butter

25 g / 1 oz flour

1 teaspoon capers

1 tablespoon lemon juice

2 tablespoons parsley, chopped

Salt and black pepper

1 lb quick flaky pastry
    (see recipe on page 41)

1 egg, beaten, to glaze

SERVES 4–6

Place the salmon into a large saucepan, cover with the milk and simmer for about 5 minutes. Strain the milk into a jug and place the salmon to one side.

Melt the butter in the saucepan and then add the flour, cook for 3 minutes and then slowly return the milk back to the saucepan, stirring all the time until the sauce thickens. Add the salmon and the rest of the ingredients, stir and allow the mixture to cool.

Make up the pastry and pre-heat the oven to 220ºC / 425ºF / gas mark 7.

Put the salmon filling into a pie casserole dish and top with the flaky pastry, crimp the edges and glaze.

Bake in the centre of the oven for 30 minutes.

Serve with new potatoes and minted peas.

Shrimp Pie

Pick a quart of shrimps.

If they be very salty, season them only with mace and a clove or two.

Bone and mince two or three anchovies, mix them with the spice, and then season the shrimps.

Put some butter at the bottom of a shallow pie dish.

Put in the shrimps, and pour over them some more butter and a glass of sharp white wine.

Cover with a very thin delicate pie crust and bake until this is cooked.

It won't take long.

This recipe from Suffolk in 1823 might have tasted nice if it hadn't been so heavy on the mace and cloves, and then topped with anchovies!

Nichola Dixon's Luxury Fish Pie

I have worked with BBC Radio many times and producer Nichola Dixon adores this fish pie, which she now cooks for her relatives in Huddersfield, so I have named it in her honour. It makes a delicious family supper, using the good old Knorr stock cube, one of my dear friend Marco Pierre White's favourite ingredients! Enjoy.

750 g / 1 lb 10 oz floury potatoes

200 g / 7 oz white fish cod

200 g / 7 oz wild salmon fillet

140 g / 5 oz naturally (un-dyed) smoked haddock

100 g / 4 oz uncooked king prawns

1 Knorr fish stock cube

225 ml / 7½ fl oz double cream

1 small leek, sliced

100 g / 4 oz fresh peas

2 hard boiled eggs, chopped

40 g / 1½ oz Cheddar cheese, grated

125 ml / 4½ fl oz milk

3 egg yolks

SERVES 4–6

Pre-heat oven to 220°C / 425°F / gas mark 7.

Cook the potatoes in boiling water until soft, then mash or pass through a sieve or potato ricer.

Check the fish for bones, cut it into chunks and place in the bottom of a large ovenproof dish with the prawns.

Pour the cream into a pan, crumble in the stock cube and bring to the boil, whisking to dissolve the cube. Pour over the fish.

At the same time, blanch the leek in boiling water for 1 minute, just to soften it a bit. Drain and immediately add to the fish with the peas. Sprinkle with the chopped eggs and cheese.

Bring the milk to the boil and add to the potatoes. Stir in, then add the egg yolks and stir to combine. Don't season your potatoes, as we already have seasoning in the cream.

Fork the mash over the top of the dish and bake for 25 minutes.

Partan Pie

This recipe, from the windy coast of Fife, slightly bends the definition of pie, but it is so tasty I just had to include it. It would have been a very messy job making it years ago, but not these days because you can buy crab meat anywhere, without the hassle of skewers and nutcrackers. I like to place the crab mixture into oyster shells or small ovenproof pie dishes. Traditionally served with oatmeal cobs and lashings of fresh butter.

450 g / 1 lb crab meat, brown and white

½ teaspoon or 1 nutmeg, freshly grated

Salt and white pepper

45 ml / 3 tablespoons white wine vinegar

30 ml / 2 tablespoons Arran mustard

75 g / 3 oz soft brown breadcrumbs

30 g / 1¼ oz butter

SERVES 4

Pre-heat the oven to 180°C / 350°F / gas mark 4.

Mix the crabmeat together and season it well with the nutmeg, salt and pepper. Mix the ingredients thoroughly.

Place the crabmeat into shells or small pie dishes.

Gently heat the vinegar and mustard together and pour over the crabmeat.

Cover the crabmeat with a layer of breadcrumbs and dot the top of the breadcrumbs with butter. Place in the centre of the oven for 15 minutes.

Devonshire Grey Mullet Pie

This is a recipe I came across in St Ives many years ago. You can use red snapper if you wish, but grey mullet is very popular in this part of Devon and has a wonderful flavour. It is nearly always poached in milk, but it has more flavour if slowly baked in a pastry crust with a white sauce.

6 medium-sized grey mullet
   fillets, bones and skin
   removed

Salt and black pepper

450 ml / ¾ pint white sauce
   using fish stock
   (see recipe on page 52)

1 tablespoon chopped parsley

250 g / 9 oz shortcrust pastry
   (see recipe on page 33)

1 egg, beaten, to glaze

SERVES 4

Pre-heat the oven 220ºC / 425ºF / gas mark 7.

Cut the fish into small pieces about 4 cm / 1½ inches.

Toss the fish in a little seasoned flour and lay in the bottom of a deep pie dish.

Make up the white sauce using fish stock.

Sprinkle the fish with chopped parsley and just cover with the sauce.

Make the pastry and roll out, keeping leftover bits for decoration. Cut a strip for the edge of the pie dish and fit the lid to this.

Crimp and seal the edges well. Make two slits in the middle of the pie.

Bake in the centre of the oven for 10 minutes.

Add decorative pastry fish shapes, glaze and continue cooking at a reduced heat of 180ºC / 350ºF / gas mark 4 for a further 30 minutes.

The Stables Brasserie Fish Pie

David and Jeanne who own the Stables Brasserie in Wigan gave me this very special recipe, which uses wild salmon and haddock poached in a creamy sauce and topped with creamed potatoes. Thanks, you two!

225 g / 8 oz each of salmon and haddock fillets, skinned

100 g / 4 oz spring onions, finely chopped

1 tablespoon lemon juice

100 g / 4 oz sliced button mushrooms

1 bay leaf

300 ml / 10 fl oz milk

25 g / 1 oz unsalted butter

25 g / 1 oz seasoned flour

450 g / 1 lb cooked potatoes, mashed with 25 g / 1 oz butter and 2 tablespoons double cream

100 g / 4 oz Lancashire cheese, grated

SERVES 4

Pre-heat the oven to 190ºC / 375ºF / gas mark 5.

Place the salmon and haddock, onions, lemon juice, mushrooms and bay leaf in a saucepan. Pour over the milk and slowly bring to the boil.

Cover and simmer for 15 minutes. Carefully remove the fish and vegetables, strain the liquid into a bowl and reserve. Discard any fish bones, along with the bay leaf.

Melt the butter in a saucepan, gradually adding the flour, and cook gently for 2 minutes, then slowly add the reserved milk. Bring to the boil and simmer for 2 minutes until the sauce thickens and becomes very smooth. Add the fish and vegetables.

Place the mixture into a shallow 1.2 litre / 2 pint ovenproof serving dish. Allow the mixture to cool and then cover completely with the creamed mashed potato, sprinkle all over with the grated cheese and bake in the centre of the oven for 30 minutes until golden brown.

Cobblers & hotpots

Cobblers and hotpots are wonderfully comforting varieties of pie which make hearty and satisfying meals. A hotpot, of course, is often topped with sliced potato, while cobblers have a savoury scone-like topping – each scone forming a separate 'cobbler'. Although both are usually made as big family-and-friends-sized affairs, they can also be made and bought as mini versions with all sorts of fillings. Either way, they make great eating and are easy and fun to cook. Of course, there are those who might say that they aren't pies at all, but I say cobblers to 'em!

Lancashire Hotpot with Potatoes or Pastry

I created this for the Richard and Judy show to celebrate Betty's Hotpot on Coronation Street!

1 kg / 2½ lb under shoulder, neck and shin of Lancashire lamb or mutton (cut into 3–4 cm / 1½–2 inch thick pieces)

35 g / 1½ oz plain flour

Freshly milled white peppercorns (optional)

700 g / 1½ lb thinly sliced red onions

20 g / ¾ oz beef dripping

1 kg / 2½ lb peeled King Edward potatoes, sliced 2 mm / ⅛ inch thick

½ teaspoon crushed rosemary

25 g /1 oz salted butter, melted

150 ml / ¼ pint chicken stock

50 ml / 3 tablespoons mild beer

3 teaspoons salt

1 lb shortcrust pastry (see recipe on page 33)

SERVES 4–6

Pre-heat the oven to 180ºC–200ºC / 350ºF–400ºF / gas mark 4–6.

Season the lamb or mutton with one teaspoon of salt and a good pinch of pepper, dust with the flour.

Put the meat into the base of a hotpot dish. Fry, but don't brown, the onions in the beef dripping with one teaspoon of salt for 4–5 mins.

Spread the onions evenly on top of the meat in the hotpot dish. Put the sliced potatoes into in a medium size bowl, add the melted butter, season with rosemary, 1 teaspoon of salt and a pinch of pepper, and mix well.

Put the sliced potatoes evenly on top of the onions, reserving the best-shaped rounds for the final layer, and add the chicken stock and beer.

Place the hotpot, covered, in the pre-heated oven for 30 minutes, then for approximately 2½ hours on 140ºC / 275ºF / gas mark 1. Remove from the oven, take off the lid or cover with more potato or shortcrust pastry, return to the oven on 180ºC–200ºC / 350ºF–400ºF / gas mark 4–6 for 30 minutes or until golden brown.

Serve with Red Velvet Beetroot, pickled red cabbage and glazed baby carrots.

Yorkshire Black Hotpot with Suet Dumplings

Several years ago, to accompany the TV series, my *Heartbeat Cookbook* was published, containing some wonderful traditional Yorkshire recipes. I wish I'd been able to include this recipe but it was not until after publication that I came across this dish, which is similar to my father's Tattie Pot except for the barley, lentils and pastry.

450 g / 1 lb rump steak, diced

2 lamb's kidneys, sinew removed, chopped

1 black pudding, skin removed and diced

50 g / 2 oz oyster mushrooms, chopped

1 large onion, chopped

1 large carrot, peeled and chopped

15 g / 2 teaspoons barley

30 g / 4 teaspoons lentils

½ teaspoon sage

Salt and black pepper

600 ml / 1 pint beef stock

100 g / 4 oz suet crust pastry (see recipe on page 35)

A little plain flour

SERVES 4–6

Pre-heat the oven 150ºC / 300ºF / gas mark 2.

Ensure all the meat is cut into generous chunks, put all the ingredients into a large oven-to-table casserole dish and cover with the beef stock and extra water if required.

Place in the centre of the oven and cook for 2 hours.

Divide the pastry into 10 pieces, each the size of a small egg. Lightly flour your hands and roll each piece into a small ball or dumpling. Place the dumplings into the casserole and cook for a further 30 minutes.

Serve with pickled red cabbage and a mustard mash potato

151

Beef Stew & Horseradish Dumplings

Beef stew is nothing less than a national institution, and to my mind it just isn't right without some lovely, spongey dumplings. You'll always find a simple version of this very British dish in supermarkets, and every region has its own version. But it's so easy to make, and cheap too, so you've no excuse not to get on with it – happy cooking!

For the stew

900 g / 2 lb Scottish shin beef, diced, fat and gristle removed

50 g / 2 oz flour, well seasoned

50 g / 2 oz beef dripping

3 onions, peeled and sliced

600 ml / 20 fl oz good quality beef stock

150 ml / 5 fl oz stout

Salt and black pepper

3 large potatoes, peeled and diced

1 large carrot, peeled and diced

175 g / 6 oz button mushrooms, sliced

175 g / 6 oz peas

Sprig of thyme

Horseradish Dumplings

125 g self-raising flour

60 g shredded beef suet

15 ml / 1 tablespoon freshly grated horseradish

Salt and black pepper

Cold water to mix

SERVES 4–6

Toss the meat in the seasoned flour, heat the dripping in a large saucepan and fry the beef and onions for 5 minutes. Add the beef stock and stout, seasoning well with salt and pepper.

Bring the contents to the boil and remove any excess scum floating on the surface. Stew for 60 minutes, then add the rest of the ingredients except the dumplings, stewing slowly for a further 60 minutes.

Meanwhile make up the dumpling mix. Sieve the flour into a mixing bowl. Stir in the suet, horseradish, salt and pepper. Carefully mix enough water to make a soft dough. Turn the dough onto a floured board and with lightly floured hands shape into balls the size of a large walnut.

Add the dumplings to the stew and cook for a further 30 minutes.

Serve with crusty, warm brown bread and a glass of real ale

Beef & Beer or Red Wine Cobbler

This winter warmer is a real treat served with warm crusty bread with plenty of butter. If you don't like using beer, replace the it with 400 ml / 14 fl oz of good-quality red wine instead.

Filling

900 g / 2 lb British stewing beef, trimmed

2 onions

2 large carrots

1 small leek

1 large stick celery

1 small parsnip

1 clove garlic

6 tablespoons oil

2 tablespoons flour

1 teaspoon salt

1 teaspoon black pepper

½ teaspoon caster sugar

1 bay leaf

600 ml / 1 pint beef stock

600 ml / 1 pint beer

Cobbler

225 g / 8 oz flour

25 g / 1 oz butter

1 teaspoon English mustard

1 tablespoon parsley

225 g / 8 oz Cheddar cheese

2 eggs

2 tablespoons milk

1 teaspoon horseradish

SERVES 4–6

Pre-heat oven to 200°C / 400°F / gas mark 6.

Trim any excess fat from the beef and cut into chunks. Peel and chop all of the vegetables.

Heat half the oil in a large saucepan. Season the flour with salt and pepper and lightly coat the pieces of beef, frying in batches until golden brown. Remove and place into a casserole dish.

Add the remaining oil and brown the vegetables, adding the caster sugar. Remove and add to the casserole dish.

Add the stock to the saucepan to de-glaze (wash off the lovely juices into the sauce!), pour into the casserole.

Add the beer and bay leaf and cook, covered, for 2 hours.

Meanwhile make up the cobbler mix. Sift the flour and salt into a mixing bowl and rub the butter and mustard in. Add the parsley and three quarters of the grated cheese.

Mix the egg, milk and horseradish together and fold into the flour mixture.

Remove the casserole from the oven, remove the bay leaf, adjust seasoning.

Divide the cobbler mixture into 8 portions and place on top of the casserole. Top with the remaining cheese, return to the oven and bake for a further 30 minutes or until golden brown.

Braised Mutton & Caper Cobbler

I owe a huge 'thank you' to Brian Turner (and the Academy of Culinary Arts and Claire Bradley at H.D. Communications) for this scrumptious dish. Brian's hearty recipe makes a brilliant mid-week supper that's delicious served on its own, or with some creamy mash to soak up the juices. Yum.

For the Stew

1 kg / 2¼ lb diced leg of mutton

2 celery stalks, halved

3 medium carrots, peeled and cut in half

½ small swede, cut into 12 chunks

6 shallots, peeled

6 small turnips, scrubbed but not peeled

10 whole black peppercorns

Salt

1 sprig rosemary

1 sprig thyme

1 litre / 1¾ pints lamb stock made with 2 good quality stock cubes

For the Cobbler top

350 g / 12 oz self-raising flour

100 g / 4 oz butter, diced

50 g / 2 oz capers, chopped

10 g / ½ oz parsley, chopped

4 spring onions, finely chopped

30 ml / 2 tablespoons plain natural yoghurt mixed with 70 ml / 5 tablespoons cold water

Black pepper

SERVES 6

Place the mutton in a large casserole or pan with the vegetables, herbs and stock.

Add peppercorns and season with salt.

Bring to the boil and simmer gently for 1 hour.

To make the cobbler rub the fat and the flour together. Stir in the capers, parsley, onions and pepper, and add enough of the yoghurt and water mix to make a soft, pliable dough.

Roll dough to 2.5 cm / 1 inch thick and cut into 12 rounds or wedges. Place on top of the mutton.

Bake at 200°C / 400°F / gas mark 6 for 20–25 minutes or until the cobbler is golden brown.

Chicken, York Ham & Mustard Cobbler

This dish is always special, and extra tasty if you use cornfed chicken thigh meat and the finest York ham, then team them with a creamy white chicken sauce and top with the mustard cobbler. Looks good and tastes even better!

Filling

650 g / 1 lb 6 oz cornfed chicken thigh meat off the bone, roughly chopped

200 ml / 7 fl oz chicken stock

300 g / 11 oz York ham diced

Pinch of salt

3 tablespoons plain flour

100 ml / 4 fl oz milk

Black pepper

Cobbler

125 g / 5 oz plain flour

15 g / ½ oz English mustard powder

Salt and white pepper

50 g / 2 oz butter

25 g / 1 oz Cheddar cheese grated

50 ml / 3 tablespoons milk to bind

SERVES 4–6

Put the chicken meat and the stock into a saucepan and bring it gently to the boil, covered, over a low heat for approx 2 minutes. Add the ham.

Stir together the flour and half of the milk in a bowl. Add remaining milk and add this thickening mixture to the saucepan while stirring. Bring to the boil over a low heat, stirring for about 2 minutes.

Taste and then season with salt and pepper. Pour the mixture into a casserole dish.

Pre-heat the oven to 200°C / 400°F / gas mark 6.

Make up the cobbler by sifting the flour, salt, pepper and mustard powder into a bowl and rubbing in the butter until the mixture resembles fine breadcrumbs. Stir in the cheese and add sufficient milk to bind. Roll out the dough on a lightly floured work surface and divide into 12 small cobbler rounds. Arrange these around the edge of the dish.

Bake for 45 minutes, until golden.

Fish Hotpot

Scotland is one of the most picturesque, unspoilt places in Europe, and these days it is developing quite a reputation for good food. Not only does the country grow and make superb products such as salmon, whisky, beef, kippers and shortbread, it is also fast becoming a centre of culinary excellence. It has certainly moved on from deep-fried Mars bars and pizzas, although you can still get those!

450 g / 1 lb salmon fillet, skinned and chopped

450 g / 1 lb hake fillet, skinned and chopped

75 g / 3 oz plain, seasoned flour

Salt and black pepper

75 g / 3 oz best butter

4 shallots, skinned and finely chopped

1 carrot, peeled and diced

1 leek, washed, and finely chopped

300 ml / ½ pint of dry white wine

300 ml / ½ pint of medium sweet cider

10 ml / 2 teaspoons anchovy essence

15 ml / 1 tablespoon tarragon vinegar

200 g / 8 oz Loch Fyne smoked mussels (optional)

Chopped fresh parsley

SERVES 4–6

Coat the fish in 25 g / 1 oz of the seasoned flour. Melt the butter in a flameproof casserole and add the fish, shallots, carrot and leek, cooking gently for 10 minutes.

Sprinkle with the remaining flour, stirring for 2 minutes.

Slowly add the wine, cider, anchovy essence and tarragon vinegar. Bring to the boil and simmer for 35 minutes on a low heat. After 25 minutes add the smoked mussels and cook for 10 minutes, or if you're not using mussels just bake the casserole in the oven for 30 minutes total, at 180°C / 350°F / gas mark 4.

Sprinkle with freshly chopped parsley and serve with warm, crusty brown bread.

You can try using wild salmon for this recipe, and for an extra boost use Loch Fyne smoked mussels too

156

Ghillie's Hotpot

This classic dish was created in early Victorian times to use up any leftover bits of game, so of course it was a very popular dish with gamekeepers. I first tasted this at a venison shoot in the early 1980s. The Lairhillock Inn in Aberdeen makes its wonderful Ghillie's Hotpot with wild boar and venison, but you can just choose a selection of what you fancy. I like a combination of venison haunch, pheasant, grouse and rabbit, myself.

50 g / 2 oz beef dripping

900 g / 2 lb mixed game meat, bones removed

2 or 3 large red onions, peeled and sliced

1 small swede, diced

1 large carrot, diced

25 g / 1 oz plain flour

600 ml / 1 pint beef stock

115 ml / 4 fl oz port

Salt and black pepper

1 tablespoon of crushed rosemary

Pinch of crushed cloves

900 g / 2 lb potatoes, peeled and thinly sliced

SERVES 6

Pre-heat the oven to 190ºC / 375ºF / gas mark 5.

Heat the dripping in a large frying pan and quickly brown the game meat, cooking for about 5 minutes.

Transfer the meat to a large ovenproof casserole, season well and keep warm in a low oven.

Fry the onions until they become transparent (about 3 minutes), add the swede, carrot and the flour and cook for 2 minutes. Slowly add the beef stock and port, season well with salt and pepper, and add the rosemary and cloves, stirring all the time.

Remove the game from the oven and layer the game meat with the potatoes.

Pour over the stock and put on a tight-fitting lid. Cook in the centre of the oven for 2 hours.

Take off the lid for the last 15 minutes to brown the potatoes.

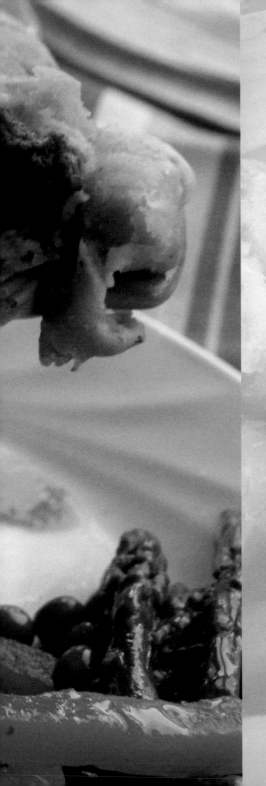

Savoury puddings

We have a wealth of savoury puddings in the UK, regularly served in the crème de la crème of hotels and restaurants throughout the country The most talked about pudding, and the best known, has to be the good old steak and kidney pud. I have had it at the Savoy, the Waldorf, Simpsons in the Strand, Rules, and Porters in London, to name but a few of the posh ones, though you can find equally good versions in much more humble establishments too, of course.

When my wife Jayne and I used to do our Christmas visit to the Cavendish Hotel in London I would say, 'Where shall we go for lunch, then?', and Jayne would smile and off we would go to Covent Garden for my yearly Porters steak and kidney pudding. Owned by Richard, Earl of Bradford, it is a pie and pudding heaven of the highest calibre – definitely worth a visit, and it doesn't even cost a fortune!

Tom's Suet Pastry & Steak & Kidney Pudding

My gran and my mother were complete artists when it came to making suet pastry. This pudding weighs in at 675 g / 1 lb 8 oz per pudding, and you will need 3 large pudding basins, 6½ cm / 2½ inches deep × 14 cm / 5½ inches wide – each should hold approximately 350 ml / 12 fl oz. You will also need tinfoil and kitchen string. Commonly known in Wigan as a Babbysyed, the nation's most famous weatherman, Fred Talbot, told me that if I ever stopped making this pudding I would no longer be welcome in the north of England! Come on Fred have a go yourself!

For the pastry

500 g / 1 lb 2 oz self-raising flour, plus a little extra

250 g /9 oz shredded suet, or vegetarian 'light' alternative

Sea salt

Approx 8 tablespoons cold water

Extra flour for rolling

Butter for lining the dishes

For the filling

1 large onion

30 ml / 2 tablespoons vegetable oil

250 g / 3 large flat mushrooms

1 kg / 2¼ lb British chuck steak

250 g / 9 oz lamb's kidneys

30 ml / 2 tablespoons flour

1 teaspoon chopped fresh thyme

Salt and black pepper

Butter

600 ml / 1 pint beef stock and 150 ml / ¼ pint port

For extra gravy

1 tablespoon soft butter

1 tablespoon flour

1 teaspoon redcurrant jelly

Salt and black pepper

SERVES 4–6

Sift the flour into a mixing bowl; add the suet and a good pinch of salt. Mix, then add the water, a little at a time, to bind into a light, spongy pastry. Rest for 20 minutes while you prepare everything else.

Halve, peel and finely chop the onion. Soften in the oil in a frying pan. Tip onto a plate to cool. Wipe the mushrooms and cut into chunky pieces.

Trim away fat and sinew from the steak and cut into kebab-size chunks or $1 \times 1 \times 3$ cm / $\frac{1}{2} \times \frac{1}{2} \times 1\frac{1}{2}$ inch strips. Cut the kidney into slightly smaller pieces, discarding the white core. Mix the meat and kidney and dust liberally with flour. Mix with the mushroom and onion. Season with salt and pepper, adding chopped thyme if liked.

Halve the pastry and flour a work surface. Lavishly butter the pudding basins. Working on one pudding at a time, set aside just over a quarter of the pastry for a lid. Roll the pastry into a circle to fit the basin with a 2 cm / 1 inch overhang. Repeat with the second pudding.

Add the filling and sufficient stock and port to moisten but not drench or cover the filling. Roll the lid to fit. Moisten the overhang, fit the lid and pinch and roll the two together to seal securely.

Pleat a large piece of tinfoil and place loosely over the top. Tie it securely, going round twice, with string under the rim of the basin, then loop a handle across the top of the pudding, allowing plenty of room for the pudding to expand — which it will.

Roll the excess foil up and over the string and lift the pudding into a large saucepan with a tight-fitting lid. Add sufficient boiling water to come two thirds of the way up the basin, fit the lid and boil for 4 hours. Check every hour or so and top up with more boiling water.

To serve, lift the pudding out of the bowl onto a plate. Remove the foil. Wrap a napkin around the basin with the top crust showing and serve from the basin with extra gravy, new and roast potatoes, peas, asparagus, cabbage and baton carrots, and English mustard and redcurrant jelly.

To make the gravy, mash the butter and flour together. Bring the leftover beef stock to the boil. Add the redcurrant jelly and scraps of butter and flour, whisking to incorporate. Taste and adjust the seasoning with salt and pepper and pour into a gravy boat or jug to serve.

A Truly Edwardian Quail & Beef Pudding, by Rosa Lewis, 1890

This classic recipe was the creation of Rosa Lewis, who purchased the Cavendish Hotel in Mayfair in 1902, and whose life story was the inspiration for the classic television series, The Duchess of Duke Street. Rosa was famous for her game sauces and quail pudding, created for her long-time friend King Edward VII, who dined regularly at the Cavendish.

Rosa was an amazing woman, especially for her time, and I reckon that she deserves to be much more widely known, so I am researching and writing about her life and recipes. I hope you enjoy this one as much as I do.

Rosa's filling

50 g / 2 oz butter

Pinch of fine herbs

12 quail breasts, skin removed

75 g / 3 oz button mushrooms

50 g / 2 oz shallots, sliced

150 ml / 5 fl oz fresh orange juice

1 sprig of fresh thyme

2 tablespoons brandy

Salt and black pepper

150 ml / 5 fl oz game sauce

450 g / 1 lb Aberdeen Angus beef, fat removed, cut into thin slices

A little melted butter

Rosa's suet crust – she always used this for her game pies and quail puddings

225 g / 8 oz self-raising flour

1 level teaspoon baking powder

Salt and white pepper

Pinch of mace

Pinch of ground rosemary

100 g / 4 oz beef suet

60 ml / 4 tablespoons approx of cold water to mix

SERVES 4–6

Melt the butter in a large frying pan, add the herbs, quail breasts, button mushrooms and shallots and pan-fry them for 6 minutes. Remove the breasts from the pan.

Add the orange juice, thyme, brandy and seasoning to the pan and simmer for at least 20 minutes until the liquid is reduced by half. Add the game sauce and simmer and reduce by half again.

To make the suet crust, sieve the flour, baking powder, herbs, spices, salt and pepper. Lightly toss in the beef suet and stir in loosely with a fork. Make a well in the centre of the mixture and add just enough water to make workable dough. Knead for a few minutes only and then the pastry is ready for immediate use.

Layer the quail meat and beef with the game sauce into a 20 cm / 8 inch pudding basin which has been buttered and lined with the suet pastry.

Cover the top of the basin with the pastry and seal; gently brush the top with melted butter and cover with several layers of cooking foil. Steam the pudding in a covered saucepan for 2 hours, topping up the pan with extra water as necessary.

Serve with fresh asparagus and duck-fat roasted potatoes.

Nineteenth-century Cheese & Onion Pudding

This is so simple to make I couldn't resist including it here. Ensure that it is seasoned well, and use free range eggs and full fat milk for a really good flavour. For even more flavour and extra filling add 25 g / 1 oz Blue Stilton, together with 100 g / 4 oz cooked macaroni, to the mixture.

600 ml / 1 pint milk

225 g / 8 oz onions

170 g / 6 oz fresh freadcrumbs

100 g / 4 oz mature cheese

3 eggs, beaten

Parsley, chopped

Salt and cayenne pepper

SERVES 4

Pre-heat oven to 200ºC / 400ºF / gas mark 6.

Peel and slice the onions thinly and gently poach in the milk in a saucepan until just tender.

Remove from the heat and allow to cool slightly.

Add the breadcrumbs, eggs, most of the cheese and the chopped parsley, seasoning to taste and mixing well.

Place into a lightly oiled, ovenproof dish, sprinkle with the remaining cheese.

Bake for 20–25 minutes.

A tale of two puddings

Simpsons Kentish Chicken Pudding

Take 2 chickens each weighing 2 ¼ lbs, 1lb salt belly of pork, 12 small button onions, chopped parsley, salt, pepper and ½ pint of water.

Partly cook pork and cut into pieces. Remove the legs from chickens and cut breasts in two. Layer the chicken, pork, onions and chopped parsley, and build up until the basin is full (first lining basin with suet paste made as previously directed), add water, and cover with suet paste. Boil for 3 hours. Serve with this, if you like, a sauce made from the liquid from stewing chicken pieces, thickened lightly with arrowroot, and then adding 1 gill of cream and a little chopped parsley.

Simpsons' Steak, Kidney, Mushroom & Oyster Pudding

For the first, which is enough for six people according to the Simpson generous tradition, you will need 3 lb stewing steak, 1 ½ lb ox kidney, 1lb mushrooms, 12 oysters, 1 chopped onion, 1 tablespoon flour, Pinch of mixed herbs, salt and pepper. For the suet paste you will need 2lb flour, 1lb chopped suet, 1 pint water, Pinch of salt.

Cut steak and kidney into equal sizes, add seasoning, chopped onion and mushrooms sliced small. Mix all together with the flour, and place in a basin already lined with suet paste. Add a teacup of water and cover the basin with remaining suet paste. Steam or boil for 3 ½ hours. Add oysters, partly cooked, before serving. Suet paste, as you do not need me to tell you, is made by mixing the flour, finely chopped suet and the salt, and then forming into a dough with the water. Roll lightly out on a floured board, and use as required.

These two scrumptious offerings are from Simpsons on the Strand in London, purveyors of superb British cuisine. Dating from 1942, when food was rationed, I made this recipe and it was really nice using beef stock instead of water.

Oxtail, Beef & Lamb's Kidney Pudding

900 g / 2 lb fresh oxtail

450 g / 1 lb beef skirt, diced into large chunks

170 g / 6 oz diced lamb's kidney

2 red onions peeled and sliced

Pinch of mace

4 sprigs of thyme

600 ml / 1 pint of real ale

300 ml / ½ pint of red wine

600 ml / 1 pint chicken stock

½ teaspoon salt and black pepper

A little melted butter

SERVES 4–6

Put all ingredients in a large pan, bring to boil and simmer for 90 minutes.

Strain the meat and vegetables and place to one side, returning the stock to the pan.

Bring the stock to the boil and simmer until it is reduced by half.

Remove the meat from the oxtail bones and add the oxtail meat to the meat and vegetables. Pour over enough stock to cover the mixture.

Line a buttered 20 cm / 8 inch pudding basin with the suet pastry. Pour in the filling.

Cover the top of the basin with suet pastry and seal; gently brush the top with melted butter and cover with several layers of cooking foil. Steam the pudding in a covered saucepan for 90 minutes, topping up the pan with extra water as necessary.

Aberdeen Angus Beefsteak Pudding

Hmmm, what to serve with this luscious beefsteak pudding … what would the readers of this book enjoy? I reckon rustic fat chips cooked in duck fat, with fresh mint peas and gravy, would be just the ticket!

1 lb suet pastry
  (see recipe on page 35)

25 g / 1 oz beef dripping

675 g / 1½ lb Aberdeen Angus rump steak, cut into chunks, fat removed

2 large red onions, finely chopped

40 g / 1½ oz plain flour

1 nutmeg, grated

425 ml / 15 fl oz rich beef stock

50 ml / 3 tablespoons port wine

Salt and black pepper

1 tablespoon chopped parsley

SERVES 4–6

Line and grease a large 1.35 kg / 3 lb pudding basin or 4 to 6 individual pudding basins with butter and the suet pastry, leaving roughly a quarter for the lid(s).

Fill a steamer with water, or a large saucepan half filled, to hold the pudding basin(s).

In a large saucepan, heat the dripping and fry the steak for 4 minutes. Add the onion, and cook for a further 2 minutes. Sprinkle with flour and nutmeg and cook for 3 minutes, then add the beef stock, port, seasoning and parsley and simmer for a further 20 minutes.

Remove the steak from the heat and allow it to cool.

Place the meat and stock into the suet-lined pudding basin(s). Roll out the lid(s) and cover the pudding(s), pressing and securing the edges with a little water.

Cover the pudding(s) with a double piece of greaseproof paper, tied down with string, leaving room for the pastry to expand.

Place into the steamer or saucepan of boiling water with a tightly closed lid and steam for 2 hours, taking great care to top up with boiling water regularly.

Let the pudding stand for ten minutes before serving Any beef stock that is left you can put into a sauce boat and serve with the pudding.

Thirty years ago Richard, Earl of Bradford had an **English pie dream**

❝Once upon a time I had a dream: to open a reasonably priced, real English restaurant in central London, not aimed at the posh end of the market, but to create somewhere with the fun atmosphere and friendly service of an American-style eatery, ensuring at the same time that it was family friendly.

When details came through for large premises in Henrietta Street, a mere 100 yards from the main market, with a glorious frontage of Victorian tiles and polished wood, it seemed ideal.

The natural English product to concentrate on, trying to compete with the Italian pizza or the American hamburger, in my view, was the pie – an infinite variety of fillings and toppings, capable of being prepared in bulk and easily served as an individual dish. The pies would be accompanied by mashed potato, and the menu would contain a wide choice of British 'nursery' puddings. We didn't look back.

Our top chefs produce this classic dish in various ways. My 'something to share' is always a big hit. In Dr Johnson's day it was a marvel in suet pastry: 'entombed there-in beefsteaks, kidneys, oysters, larks, mushrooms and wondrous spices and gravies, the secret of which is only known to the compounder'.❞

Visit www.porters.co.uk for more information.

Scotland's Own Teviotdale Pie

This really is a pie-lover's favourite, and very popular around the UK at the moment, not only in households but also in restaurants, cafes and hotels. Originating in the Scottish borders, minced beef was often used, with vegetables, but to achieve the perfect pie make sure you use best Aberdeen Angus rump steak and ox kidney. Of course, it is the suet batter that really makes it taste so good!

575 g / 1¼ lb rump steak, cubed, skin and fat removed

175 g / 6 oz ox kidney (optional)

1 large red onion

600 ml / 1 pint beef stock with beer

25 g / 1 oz seasoned flour

25 g / 1 oz butter

Salt and black pepper

Suet batter mix

225 g / 8 oz self-raising flour

75 g / 3 oz fresh beef suet

30 g / 1½ oz corn flour

300 ml / ½ pint fresh milk

Salt and black pepper

SERVES 6

Pre-heat the oven to 180°C / 350°F / gas mark 4.

Remove the fat, skin and core from the kidney and dice this quite small.

Toss the steak and kidney in the seasoned flour.

In a large frying pan melt the butter, add the meat and quickly seal it all over, adding the chopped onion and cooking for 4 minutes.

Add the beef stock, season, and simmer for a further hour.

While the beef is simmering make up the suet batter. Put the self-raising flour, suet and corn flour into a large bowl, season well and slowly add the milk, whisking it until it forms a thick batter consistency.

Put the steak, kidney and stock into a 1.2 litre / 2 pint basin or pie dish and cover with the suet batter mixture. Bake in the centre of the oven for 35 to 40 minutes.

To make a steak and ale version simply omit the kidney and soak the steak in half a pint of beer overnight, then use the beer with the stock

Mrs Beeton On Beef-steak & Kidney Pudding, 1861

Ingredients – 2 lbs. of rump-steak, 2 kidneys, seasoning to taste of salt and black pepper, suet crust made with milk (see Pastry), in the proportion of 6 oz. of suet to each 1 lb. of flour.

Mode – Procure some tender rump steak (that which has been hung a little time), and divide it into pieces about an inch square, and cut each kidney into 8 pieces. Line the dish (of which we have given an engraving) with crust made with suet and flour in the above proportion, leaving a small piece of crust to overlap the edge. Then cover the bottom with a portion of the steak and a few pieces of kidney; season with salt and pepper (some add a little flour to thicken the gravy, but it is not necessary), and then add another layer of steak, kidney, and seasoning. Proceed in this manner till the dish is full, when pour in sufficient water to come within 2 inches of the top of the basin. Moisten the edges of the crust, cover the pudding over, press the two crusts together, that the gravy may not escape, and turn up the overhanging paste. Wring out a cloth in hot water, flour it, and tie up the pudding; put it into boiling water, and let it boil for at least 4 hours. If the water diminishes, always replenish with some, hot in a jug, as the pudding should be kept covered all the time, and not allowed to stop boiling. When the cloth is removed, cut out a round piece in the top of the crust, to prevent the pudding bursting, and send it to table in the basin, either in an ornamental dish, or with a napkin pinned round it. Serve quickly.

Time – For a pudding with 2 lbs. of steak and 2 kidneys allow 4 hours.

Average cost, 2s. 8d.

Sufficient for 6 persons.

Seasonable all the year, but more suitable in winter.

Note – Beef-steak pudding may be very much enriched by adding a few oysters or mushrooms. The above recipe was contributed to this work by a Sussex lady, in which county the inhabitants are noted for their savoury puddings. It differs from the general way of making them, as the meat is cut up into very small pieces and the basin is differently shaped: on trial, this pudding will be found far nicer, and more full of gravy, than when laid in large pieces in the dish.

Taken from Anthology of Puddings by Irene Veal, published by John Gifford, London in 1942.

Veggie pies

I might be a confirmed and very enthusiastic meat-eater but
I do enjoy a really good vegetable pie. And if you're a fan of
vegetarian meat alternatives you can still use the recipes in this
book, omitting the meat and using soya, quorn etc., with a bit of
extra seasoning (not just salt and pepper, mind; think mushroom
ketchup, infused oils, vinegar or even lemon juice) and maybe the
addition of a bit of good cheese.

Shirley's Summer Vegetable Pies

1 red pepper

1 yellow pepper

1 yellow courgette

1 green courgette

1 small aubergine

12 asparagus, spears

1 large tomato

12 small vine tomatoes, halved

Olive oil infused with basil

Fresh basil leaves

125 ml / 4½ fl oz tomato puree

Chilli balsamic syrup

1 vegetable stock cube

Salt and black pepper

1 kg / 2¼ lb shortcrust pastry
    (see recipe on page 33)

1 egg, beaten, to glaze

Cut the 4 peppers into chunky squares and remove seeds and skin with a sharp knife. Slice courgettes, aubergine and asparagus diagonally into 2.5 cm / 1 inch thick pieces. Cut the tomatoes into 1 cm / ½ inch squares and remove the seeds.

Heat a large griddle pan and add a little oil. Gently cook all the vegetables until they are just crisp to the bite Take the pan off the heat and add the tomato puree, basil leaves, 3 sprinkles of balsamic syrup and a vegetable stock cube. Season to taste with salt and pepper. Stir the filling well, and then set it aside to cool.

Pre-heat the oven to 180°C / 350°F / gas mark 4.

Prepare the pastry and roll out on a floured surface to 5 mm / ¼ inch thick. Cut out six large circles to fit in the pie tins and six smaller circles for the lids.

Line the tins with the large circles of pastry and divide the vegetable filling equally between the pie tins.

Cover the tops with the remaining circles of pastry. Make a small hole in the centre of each pie.

Glaze with beaten egg and place the pies onto a baking sheet.

Bake for 35 minutes in the centre of the oven.

Another recipe from Shirley's homemade pies, read all about her on page 194

Roast Winter Vegetable Pudding

This is one of the recipes I use whenever I have vegetarian friends over, although it is also a great accompaniment to any roasted meat dish. Season well and enjoy a big helping of comfort pie.

1 teaspoon fresh thyme

1 teaspoon fresh rosemary

1 teaspoon fresh sage

1–2 cloves garlic

340 g / 12 oz pumpkin or squash, peeled and deseeded

225 g / 8 oz parsnips, cut into quarters

2 large carrots, cut into quarters

2 red onions, cut into quarters

2 leeks, cut into chunks

2 potatoes, cut into wedges

1 small swede, cut into chunks

1 small celeriac, cut into chunks

1 teaspoon coriander powder

Olive oil

Salt and black pepper

1 vegetable stock cube

300 ml / ½ pint chopped tomatoes

1½ lb Rosa Lewis suet pastry (see recipe on page 35)

A little melted butter

SERVES 4–6

Pre-heat oven to 200°C / 400°F / gas mark 6.

Crush the garlic cloves and chop the herbs.

Place all of the ingredients except the tomatoes in a bowl, pour over a little olive oil and season to taste. Mix thoroughly, ensuring all vegetables are lightly coated with oil.

Arrange in a single layer on a baking tray, sprinkled with a vegetable stock cube. Roast for 20 minutes and then place the tray to one side. Pour over the chopped tomatoes, mix all the vegetables together.

Make up the suet pastry ready for immediate use and line a 20 cm / 8 inch buttered pudding basin.

Place the vegetables and juices into the lined basin. Cover the top of the basin with pastry and seal. Gently brush the top with melted butter and cover with several layers of cooking foil. Steam the pudding in a covered saucepan for 2 hours, topping up the pan with extra water as necessary.

Roasted Root Vegetable Cobbler

This really is worth the hard work of making a creamy tomato soup to pour over the vegetables before baking.

225 g / 8 oz carrots, cut into chunks

350 g / 12 oz swede, diced

350 g / 12 oz parsnips, diced

450 g / 1 lb leeks, sliced

225 g / 8 oz sweet potato, diced

150 ml / ¼ pint vegetable stock

Olive oil

295 g / 10 oz cream of tomato soup

A little milk

1 lb Cobbler pastry
(see recipe on page 42)

Tomato soup

2 onions, peeled and chopped

1 carrot, peeled and diced finely

1 stick celery, finely chopped

1 clove garlic, peeled and crushed

2 tablespoons olive oil

650 g /1 lb 6 oz fresh ripe vine tomatoes, halved

1 teaspoon sugar

Salt and black pepper

1 litre / 1¾ pints vegetable stock

SERVES 6

Pre-heat the oven to 200°C / 400°F / gas mark 6.

Mix all the vegetables together and arrange them in a non-stick roasting tin. Pour in the stock and sprinkle the vegetables with the olive oil. Roast in the oven for 20 minutes.

Mix the soup with the vegetables and spoon the mixture into an ovenproof dish.

Make up the cobbler pastry and roll out the dough on a lightly floured surface to a thickness of about 1 cm / ½ inch. Cut out rounds with an 7½ cm / 3 inch cutter (or a cup or glass with the same diameter) and arrange them around the edge of the dish. Brush the cobbler with the milk.

Bake in the centre of the oven for 20–25 minutes until the cobbler topping is risen and golden.

Serve with wholemeal crusty bread

Tomato soup

Heat the oil in a large saucepan and add the onions, carrot and celery and garlic. Cover and cook gently for 10 minutes until soft.

Add the tomatoes, sugar, salt, pepper and tomatoes. Stir and cook for another 5 minutes.

Add the stock, bring to the boil and simmer for 10 minutes. Liquidise until smooth.

Heather's Super Vegetarian Slice

I tasted this at Wigan Food Festival and I must say that 15-year-old schoolgirl Heather has created the most wonderful flavour and texture I have ever tasted in a vegetable pie. The shredded shitake gives the pie a great 'veggie-meat'-style flavour. It was awesome, and thanks go to Heather for sharing it with the nation! As Heather says:

> The reason I like making this vegetable slice is because I like to experiment with different ingredients, and it is different from a lot of pies you can buy from shops. I think that the colours and texture of the slice also make it stand out from others. I also think that it is very versatile as it can be eaten hot or cold, yet still keeps enough of its flavour. It can be a main meal, a snack or even finger food for parties. I also like helping my dad make it for his friends.

450 g / 1 lb Maris Piper potatoes, peeled and diced

1 onion, peeled and chopped

1 red pepper, diced

125 g / 4½ oz broccoli florets

150 g / 5 oz carrots, diced

250 g / 9 oz shitake mushrooms, shredded

1 clove of garlic, chopped

15 ml / 1 tablespoon olive oil

100 g / 4 oz tomato puree

1 oxo vegetable stock cube

3 dashes Tabasco sauce

Salt and black pepper

450 g / 1 lb shortcrust pastry (see recipe on page 33)

SERVES 4–6

Pre-heat the oven 180°C / 350°F / gas mark 4.

Slowly steam the potatoes, carrots and broccoli until just tender.

Soften the onion, pepper and mushrooms in a frying pan with a little olive oil, with the crushed clove of garlic. Add the tomato puree and crumble a stock cube onto the mix (don't add any liquid). Add the Tabasco sauce and pepper and mix gently over a low heat so you don't break up the vegetables.

Roll out half of your pastry and place onto a shallow baking tray. Add your mixture and then place over the top the other half of your rolled out pastry. Cook in the centre of the oven for 25 minutes.

Silly pies!

Most of my pies are pretty sensible really: not too many wacky ingredients or difficult methods. And that's what an everyday pie should be like. But that doesn't mean that every now and then we can't indulge in a bit of fantasy pie-making, using slightly more outlandish ingredients and making a bit more effort. So this short section is dedicated to a bit of pie daftness – something I'm very partial to – and I dare you to make one!

The perfect Wedding Pie from Wilson's of Leeds

Hand-raised Gold Leaf Game Pie

I made this ridiculously expensive pie to be auctioned off to raise funds for Derian House Children's Hospice. It cost £1,700 all told, because of the truffle, champagne and gold leaf used, so you probably wouldn't want to fork out that much! It's fun to read about, though, and you could make it with some nice wild mushrooms, wine and no gold leaf – but then it wouldn't be such a silly pie would it!!

Ingredients for the pie filling

1 partridge

2 pheasant and grouse

500 g / 1 lb 2 oz loins of rabbit

1 pig's foot

1 carrot, chopped

1 stick celery

sprig thyme

sprig rosemary

2 onions, chopped

125 ml / 4½ fl oz white wine

450 g / 1 lb venison shoulder

1 kg / 2¼ lb Cumbrian Sausage meat

1 clove garlic, crushed

1 tablespoon tarragon

125 ml / 4½ fl oz champagne

100 g / 4 oz Umbrian black truffle

Pinch mace

6 juniper berries, crushed

4 sheets of gold leaf

SERVES 8–10

For the hot water truffle butter crust pastry

Butter, for greasing

110 g / 4½ oz truffle butter

280 ml / 9 fl oz water

500 g / 1 lb 2 oz plain flour, plus extra for dusting

2 teaspoons salt

1 egg, beaten, to glaze

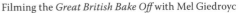

Filming the *Great British Bake Off* with Mel Giedroyc

Pre-heat the oven to 200°C / 400°F / gas mark 6.

For the pie filling: take the meat off the partridges, pheasant, grouse and rabbit loins and reserve the bones for making the stock.

Place the bones in a large pot, followed by the pig's foot, carrot, celery, thyme, rosemary, and half of the onion. Pour in the white wine and add enough cold water to just cover the bones. Bring to boil and simmer for about 2 hours, skimming off any scum on the surface with a ladle.

While the stock is simmering, mix together the sausage meat, the rest of the onion, the crushed garlic, and tarragon in a bowl. Roughly chop the game meats and stir into the mixture, then season well with salt and pepper. Sprinkle over the champagne, mace and crushed juniper berries. Mix well and set aside.

For the hot water truffle crust pastry: lightly grease a 20 cm cake tin and put in the fridge for 15–20 minutes to firm up the butter.

In a saucepan, add the truffle butter and water and bring to the boil, stirring constantly.

Sieve the flour into a large bowl and add the salt. Make a well in the middle of the flour and add the hot truffle butter and water mixture, mixing together quickly with a wooden spoon to form a dough. Cover with cling film and leave to rest for 20 minutes.

Lightly flour your work surface and roll out two thirds of the dough, reserving the final third for the pie lid. Use the pastry to line the cake tin and spoon the meat mixture evenly into the pie.

Roll the remaining pastry dough into a piece large enough to cover the cake tin, and cut a circle the size of a £2 coin in the middle.

Using a pastry brush, lightly coat the edges of the pie with the beaten egg and lay the dough lid over the pie. Crimp the edges, and glaze.

Place the pie on a baking tray and bake in the oven for 30 minutes, then lower the oven to 180°C / 350°F / gas mark 4 and bake for a further 1½ hours, until the top of the pie is golden brown. Remove from the oven and allow to almost cool completely.

Take the stock off the heat and strain through a sieve. Return to the stove and reduce the stock to approximately half a pint. Allow the stock to cool slightly, and then pour through the hole in the top of the pie and place in the fridge to set overnight.

Cover with gold leaf.

Traditional Christmas Pye

This is a recipe from the eighteenth century that I have updated for the British Christmas. The pie would originally have had the boned poultry and game one inside the other, including turkey, goose, chicken, pigeon and quail, sausage meat, and hard boiled eggs, all in a double-thick pastry crust. Quite expensive by today's standards, but I'm sure it was worth every sixpence.

50 g / 2 oz butter

1 large onion, finely chopped

175 g / 6 oz button mushrooms

175 g / 6 oz of the following roughly chopped cooked meats: turkey, goose, chicken and York ham

Salt and black pepper

6 tablespoons brandy

300 ml / 10 fl oz turkey stock

1 teaspoon cornflour blended with a tablespoon of port

150 ml / 5 fl oz double cream

350 g / 12 oz shortcrust pastry (see recipe on page 33)

175 g / 6 oz sausage meat

4 hard boiled eggs, shelled

1 egg, beaten, to glaze

SERVES 8–10

Pre-heat the oven to 190ºC / 375ºF / gas mark 5.

In a large saucepan melt the butter; add the onion and mushrooms, cooking for 4 minutes, then add the meats and cook for a further 8 minutes.

Season well, add the brandy and turkey stock, simmer for 10 minutes, add the cornflour and double cream and simmer for 2 minutes. Remove from the heat and allow to cool.

Roll out the pastry on a lightly floured surface, use two-thirds to line a 1.4 litre / 2½ pint pie dish. Place the sausage meat on the bottom, line with the hard boiled eggs then the cooled meat mixture.

Roll out the remaining pastry and cover the pie, pressing gently to seal all round. Brush the pie with beaten egg and decorate with the trimmings and bake in the centre of the oven for 45–50 minutes.

A medieval feast

In medieval times is wasn't unusual for feasts to have 20 courses, featuring swan, grouse, pheasant, herons, larks and the peacock royal. The peacock always took centre stage on the tables of wealthy nobles, yet it was tough and tasteless, and like most game birds it should have been hung well and marinated, which they did not consider at that time.

At several of these feasts six birds were put, Russian-doll style, inside one goose, all the internal birds having been boned, and various forcemeats were layered between each bird. Lark and duck tongues, together with the livers from each bird, were placed into a pestle and mortar with various herbs, fruit and breadcrumbs, to make forcemeats, or what today we call stuffing.

Interestingly, this multi-bird dish has recently returned to our festive tables in the form of a three- or four-bird roast, particularly at Christmas and Easter. This may not be quite as grand, or the birds quite as exotic, as the traditional recipe, but as with the medieval version, each bird is bone-free, except the outer one, usually a goose or turkey, and each bird is filled or lined with a fruit or other stuffing.

Baked in a pie: a celebration of local produce at Bolton Food Market

The bustling market town of Bolton has a long heritage that stretches back to the thirteenth century, and the current market on Ashburner Street has been operating since the 1930s. It beat off stiff competition to be named the Best Indoor Market in Britain in 2010 by the National Association of British Market Authorities (NABMA). Renowned for its fresh fish, meat, poultry, offal and exotic fruit stalls, Bolton Market has won a great deal of praise for the high quality and wide variety of the produce available.

The market's popularity has grown in the last year with the addition of an in-house cookery demonstration kitchen, believed to be the first of its kind in the country. Local chefs like myself and celebrity chefs including the Hairy Bikers have cooked up dishes for the public to try in the demonstration kitchen, and many more events are planned for the coming years. With 2.5 million visitors a year shopping at Bolton Market it's certainly worth coming down to see what everyone is talking about. As Jackie Casey, who has worked for there for 11 years, says 'Bolton Market is about local people and local produce all at a local market and I would invite everybody to come and have a look.'

Take a look at the celebration pies I made for the Best Indoor Market in Britain. From left: Jeremy Bradin (award sponsor KPR), David Farmer (President National Association of British Market Authorities), Jackie Casey (Bolton Markets Manager) and the Mayor and Mayoress, Cllr Norman Critchley and his wife, Delyse.

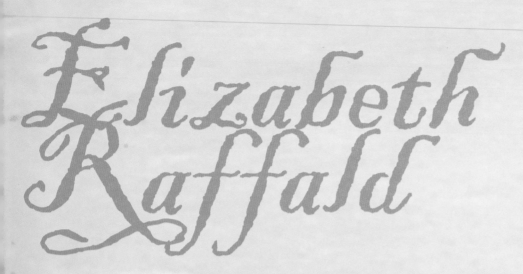

Elizabeth Raffald

A businesswoman and writer, Elizabeth Raffald (1733–81) was mother to 6 children. Born in Doncaster, she worked as housekeeper to several families, the last of which, Arley Hall in Cheshire, was where she met and married the gardener, John Raffald.

They moved to Manchester in 1763, where she kept a confectioner's shop while her husband ran a market stall. They took over the Bull's Head Inn in the market place, and later the King's Head Inn in Salford. Here she developed her culinary skills, training young ladies, collecting and inventing recipes and publishing *The Experienced English Housekeeper* – an instant success, reprinted many times and much copied, it made her a wealthy woman.

In Manchester she also opened the first Registry for Servants, compiled her *Directory of Manchester* and wrote a book on midwifery. She died in 1781 and is buried at Stockport Parish Church.

Elizabeth Raffald was also famous in connection with the Eccles cake. Although no eighteenth-century, and only a few nineteenth-century, cookery books give recipes specifically for Eccles cakes, it seems likely that early ones differed from those known today. Mrs Raffald's original recipe for 'sweet patties' of 1769 was a mixture of the meat of a boiled calf's foot (gelatine), plus apples, oranges, nutmeg, egg yolk, currants and French brandy enveloped in a good puff pastry which could be either fried or baked. The use of the word 'meat' (or 'mincemeat') in the early recipes serves as a reminder that meat was originally an ingredient in mincemeat. The fact that Eccles cakes were being exported by 1818 also suggests very good keeping qualities, so they may well have included spirits such as brandy and rum. No wonder the Puritans wanted to ban them!

What really excited me, however, was the recipe (opposite) from her famous cookbook.

A Yorkshire Goose Pie that would have cost a fortune to make ...

Take a large fat goose, split it down the back and take all the bones out. Bone a turkey and two **ducks** the same way, season them well with pepper and salt, with six woodcocks. Lay the **goose** down on a clean dish, with skin side down, and lay the **turkey** into the goose with the skin down. Have ready a large hare cleaned well, cut into pieces, and stewed in the oven with a **pound of butter**, a quarter of an ounce of mace beat fine, the same of white pepper and salt to taste, till the **meat will leave the bones**. Scum the butter of the gravy, pick the meat clean off and beat it in a **marble mortar** very fine with the butter you took off, and lay it in the turkey.

Take twenty-four pounds of the **finest flour**, six pounds of butter, half a pound of fresh rendered suet, make the paste pretty stiff and raise the pie oval. Roll out a lump of paste and cut it in **vine leaves**, or what form you please, rub the pie with yolks of eggs and put on your ornaments on the walls. Then turn the hare, turkey, and goose upside down and lay them in your pie, with the ducks at each end and the woodcocks on the sides, make your lid pretty thick and put it on. You may lay **flowers or the shape of fowls** in paste on the lid, and make a hole in the middle of your lid. The walls of the pie are to be one inch and a half higher than the lid. Then rub it all over with the yolks of eggs, and bind it round with three-fold paper, and lay the same over the top. It will take four hours baking in a brown bread oven. When it comes out melt two pounds of butter in the gravy that comes from the hare and pour it hot in the pie through a tun dish (funnel), close it well up, and let it be **eight or ten days** before you cut it. If you send it any distance make up the hole in the middle with cold butter to prevent the air from getting in.

The Ultimate Game Bird Pie

This is without doubt the tastiest pie ever, and is well worth the 48 hours (sorry!) that you have to put into making such a mouth-watering savoury.

It is my twist on the many-birded, feast centrepiece of medieval England, and uses only the finest British ingredients. The birds I use are organic and free range, and I use sausage meat mixed with chopped pork and duck livers.

Pie Ingredients

For the main pie ingredients I am using boneless meats cut into 5 cm / 2 inch dice, which are readily available from your game butcher.

450 g / 1 lb each of the following diced meat: turkey, wild duck, grouse, pheasant, partridge and guinea fowl

450 g / 1 lb pork cut into 2 cm / 1 inch dice

225 g / 8 oz sausage meat

225 g / 8 oz duck livers, trimmed, sinews removed and finely chopped

450 g / 1 lb shallots, very finely chopped

5 ml / 1 teaspoon thyme

5 ml / 1 teaspoon ground cinnamon

5 ml / 1 teaspoon sage

5 ml / 1 teaspoon crushed garlic

30 ml / 2 tablespoons parsley

15 ml / 1 tablespoon coarse sea salt

10 ml / 2 teaspoons coarse ground black pepper

80 ml / 3½ fl oz brandy

150 ml / 5 fl oz port wine

150 ml / 5 fl oz Madeira

300 ml / 10 fl oz game stock

225 g / 8 oz real Lancashire black pudding

1 egg, beaten, to glaze

SERVES 8–10

First make your game stock with all the bones and leftovers from the birds, plus one pig's foot (see page 50 for guidance).

Place all the ingredients except the black pudding into a large bowl and mix thoroughly together. Place the pie mixture into a fridge for 24 hours.

Make up the hot water pastry as shown on page 36. Roll out the pastry and pat two-thirds of the pastry into the base and around the pie dish evenly distributed to make the shape. Reserve the rest of the hot water pastry for the top.

Pre-heat the oven to 190°C / 375°F / gas mark 5.

Drain the meat in a colander, keeping the liquid.

Place the pie case onto a baking tray and put in the meat mixture into the lined pie dish. Pour on a little of the liquid. Cut the black pudding into dice and sprinkle over the mixture. Top with the pastry lid, firmly crimping the edges, being very careful not to break the pie case. Make a hole in the centre of the lid to allow the steam out during the cooking process. Bake in the lower part of the oven for 2 hours.

Meanwhile strain the liquid into a saucepan, bring to the boil and simmer for 45 minutes, then allow to cool.

10 minutes before the cooking time, glaze the pie and return to the oven.

Turn the oven off without opening the door and leave the pie in to dry naturally for 1 hour. Reheat the game stock until just warm and pour into the hole of the pie, as much stock as the pie will hold.

Let the pie cool and wrap in cling film, refrigerate for at least 24 hours to allow the pie to mature.

The Ultimate Game Bird Terrine

Use all the same ingredients and method as for the Ultimate Game Bird Pie except replace the pastry with two 28 × 11 × 8.5 cm / 11 × 4½ × 3½ inch terrine dishes or loaf tins.

Pre-heat the oven to 170°C / 325°F / gas mark 3.

Completely line these with foil, ensuring that the foil hangs over the edges.

Line each dish or tin with 225 g / 8 oz Parma ham, thinly sliced, saving 50 g / 2 oz for the top of the terrines.

Pour in the mixture and cover with Parma ham. Fold over the foil.

Place the terrines into a deep roasting pan; fill the pan with hot water to come halfway up the sides of the terrines.

Cook for 2 hours, allow to cool naturally then refrigerate for 24 hours.

Ease out the foil and slice the terrine. Serve with a fresh Red Velvet beetroot salad.

Portable pie

OK, so far all the pies in this book have been big family affairs, meant for sharing. Now it's time to sink our teeth into the portable pie, built for keeping all to yourself, and for eating on the hoof! Whether you want to munch a complete meal on the street, warm your hands at a footie match, or just enjoy an individual pie at home, you can't beat these little beauties. There are some great off-the-peg versions on the market from the likes of Pukka, Potts and Dickinson & Morris, ideal for buying when you're on the move, but I reckon you still can't beat a lovely homemade, well-filled, pastry-clad little package. From sausage rolls to pasties, the possibilities are endless, and really only limited by your imagination. Here are some cracking recipes to start you off.

The Ultimate Brit Sausage Roll

Actually I'm being a bit naughty here, because although this particular recipe is very British, the origins of the good old sausage roll are to be found in the French *saucisson brioche,* which our wealthy ancestors noticed and hugely enjoyed while travelling on the continent. You can still find different styles of them in Brittany, and I must admit that I am a big fan, especially when wrapped in crepes.

450 g / 1 lb Cumberland sausage meat or sausages (skin removed)

½ teaspoon English mustard powder

30 g / 1 oz chopped parsley

60 g / 2 oz minced red onion

Salt and black pepper

1 lb puff pastry
(see recipe on page 39)

1 egg, beaten, to glaze

MAKES ABOUT 8

Pre-heat the oven to 200ºC / 400ºF / gas mark 6.

In a clean bowl mix together the sausage meat, mustard powder, parsley, onion and seasoning. Roll out the pastry to a large rectangle about 0.25 cm / ⅛ inch in thickness and cut into half lengthways. With wet hands roll the sausage meat mixture into 2 long sausages the same length as the pastry.

Place the mixture down the centre of each piece of pastry. Dampen the edge of each strip and bring the pastry over the sausage meat, carefully pressing the edges together, ensuring the join is underneath the sausage roll.

Brush the pastry with the beaten egg. Cut into 5 cm / 2 inch lengths, and put two slits into each sausage roll. Place them carefully, well apart from each other, onto a baking sheet and bake in the centre of the oven for 20–25 minutes. Allow them to cool and serve with pickle.

For a special sausage roll lightly brush the pastry with English mustard before you add your sausage meat

My Individual Balti Pies with vegetable crisps & balti sauce

Curry pies have taken off big time in Great Britain recently. For example, the balti pie, which premiered at the grounds of Walsall and Aston Villa, is now sold at over 85 football clubs across the land. I have to admit here and now that the best chicken balti pie I have tasted so far is made by Pukka, but this is my version, in which I use thigh meat, from cornfed chickens, if possible.

450 g / 1 lb chicken thigh meat (off the bone)

Zest and juice of 1 lime

400 g / 14 oz Greek style yogurt

1 teaspoon ground turmeric

Pinch of salt

1 teaspoon sesame oil

1 large potato, washed, but not peeled, cut into 2 cm / ³/₄ inch cubes

200 ml / 7 fl oz chicken stock

Balti sauce

60 ml / 4 tablespoons sesame oil

4 onions, chopped

2 ripe tomatoes, chopped

8 cardamom pods (pre-roasted if you like)

1 teaspoon garam masala

1 teaspoon ground turmeric

1 teaspoon ground paprika

1 teaspoon chilli powder

1 teaspoon ground cumin

4 cm / 1½ inch piece fresh root ginger, peeled and grated

2 garlic cloves, crushed

2 mild green chillies, finely chopped

1 teaspoon garam masala

3 tablespoons fresh coriander, roughly chopped

450 g / 1 lb shortcrust pastry (see recipe on page 33)

450 g / 1 lb puff pastry (see recipe on page 39)

1 egg, beaten, to glaze

MAKES 6

Remove any skin and sinews from the chicken thigh meat and cut into 3 cm / 1 inch pieces.

To make the balti, marinate the chicken in the lime zest and juice, yogurt, turmeric and salt for 30 minutes.

Heat the sesame oil in a wok or frying pan and fry the potato cubes until just golden.

Add the onion, fresh tomato, cardamom pods, garam masala, turmeric, paprika, chilli powder, ground cumin, fresh ginger, and a couple of bay leaves. Stir together well, add the chicken stock and cook for about 20 minutes until slightly reduced and thickened. Remove the sauce from the heat.

Brown the chicken in a large hot wok then add the onions and stir-fry for 3–4 minutes until lightly browned. Add half the balti sauce and stir together. Add the cherry tomatoes, grated ginger and garlic. Fold in the green chillies and garam masala and stir through the coriander. Allow the mixture to cool completely.

Pre-heat the oven to 200°C / 400°F / gas mark 6.

Prepare the shortcrust pastry. Prepare the puff pastry, or take bought packet out of the fridge.

Roll out the shortcrust pastry on a floured surface to 5 mm / ¼ inch thick and cut out six large circles to fit in the pie tins. Line the tins with the shortcrust pastry.

Divide the balti filling equally into the pie tins. Roll out the puff pastry and cover the pie dishes, sealing and crimping the pastry all around.

Trim off any excess pastry and use to decorate.

Brush with egg and bake in the centre of the oven for 40 to 45 minutes.

In praise of the Butter Pie

Butter pies can be found the country over but originated in the North West, apparently invented for Lancashire's Catholic workers to eat on non-meat days, usually Fridays. Those of us with a long memory can recall them being known as Friday pies, or even Catholic pies, although these days they are often marketed as vegetarian pies, and very popular they are too.

At the Wigan Food Festival in 2010 I was with food critic and wine buff Jilly Goolden, who had never tasted – or even heard of – a butter pie, so I just had to convert her! I think I might have succeeded because she emailed me the following day to say that the fabled butter pie was 'a wonderful vegetarian option, full of flavour and must be one of the finest pies I have ever tasted'.

I knew Shirley Roberts was a kindred spirit the minute I sampled her beautiful butter pie. I was a goner from the first mouthful and became an instant fan of the mouthwatering products of Shirley's Homemade, the small but busy company she founded:

> I started making pies in my kitchen 10 years ago and did my first farmers' market at Clitheroe Auction Mart. I took along 10 pies and was amazed when they sold. I then turned my garage into a bakery, grew out of that and had an extension built on the side of my house (which, incidentally, is now the biggest dog kennel in the world!!). I grew out of that and now have a barn conversion on farmland in Pilling, near Preston, and we do about 25 markets and shows a month.

To find out more about this lovely local producer and her range, visit www.shirleyshomemade.com.

Shirley Robert's Preston North End Butter Pie. This truly deserves to be on the terraces and everywhere else too. Just look at the depth and how thin the slices of potato are in this filling

Shirley's Butter Pie

4 large potatoes

1 large onion

125 g / 4½ oz butter cut into thin flakes

450 g / 1 lb rich shortcrust pastry (see recipe on page 33)

Salt and white pepper

1 egg, beaten, to glaze

SERVES 6

Pre-heat the oven to 180ºC / 350ºF / gas mark 4.

Peel the potatoes and onion, cut the potato into very thin slices and the onion into half rings. Parboil the potatoes until they are just soft but still holding their shape, drain and place to one side. Sweat the onions off in a little butter until soft and translucent.

Prepare the pastry and roll out on a floured surface to 5 mm / ¼ inch thick. Cut out six large circles to fit in the pie tins and six smaller circles for the lids. Line the tins with the large circles.

Layer onto the pastry lining the potatoes, onions, and butter flakes, season with salt and pepper and topping off with a pastry lid. Glaze with beaten egg and place the pies onto a baking sheet. Bake for 35 minutes in the centre of the oven.

On the terraces

I really can't think of a better use for a hand-held pie than as football terrace fodder. What else can so easily be held and eaten as you sit, often shivering your socks off, watching your favourite team do their stuff? Nearly all clubs have their favourite suppliers, often local pie-makers, and more often than not the pies are offered hot, warming your hands, tum and cockles, all at once!

Without doubt one of the most famous suppliers to the terraces is Pukka Pies, which Chairman Trevor Storer started in his own kitchen in the 1960s. His first creation was their steak and kidney pie, and Trevor's wife Valerie produced the recipe for the chicken and mushroom pie, the recipes for both of which are exactly the same today. Trevor baked the pies on Mondays, Wednesdays and Fridays and sold them on Tuesdays, Thursdays and Saturdays. His company now sells a staggering 60 million pies a year and employs 280 people! Visit www.pukkapies.co.uk for more about their story and products.

Of all the terrace pies, however, the best, according to Tom Dickinson of *The Times*, is the one to be found at Morecambe FC's football ground. Said the pie-mad Mr Dickinson: 'The daddy of all pie-makers, Potts' Pies, provide the perfect mix of piping-hot meaty goodness and crisp pastry'. And after spending a day tasting their wares, I couldn't agree more! Owner Russell Walsh, like me, measures the quality of a pie by its filling and keeps a chart on his wall showing the fillings of his competitors, in order of merit. Bottom of this list is a very well-known high street chain, which shall remain nameless, but I reckon we all know who they are! You can order Potts' pies online, to be baked at home, at www.pottspies.co.uk.

But one of the oldest and most familiar of British pie makers has to be Hollands, they of the iconic green, red and gold livery, still used on all their vans. A long-time chip shop favourite in the North West of England, the company has been baking since 1851 and these days is known throughout the country. Unashamedly traditional, Hollands specialises in good old proper pies and puds, continuing to produce its perennially popular traditional range of portable pies. For more info, visit www.hollandspies.co.uk.

And another firm favourite on the terraces and streets are Peter's Pies, playing for Team Wales on the UK map of pie makers! They've been around for a bit too, over 50 years in fact, which is even more evidence, if any were needed, of the British love of a good pie. Peter's pies are of the old fashioned, time-honoured variety, and you can find out all about them at www.petersfood.co.uk.

Andrew and Tim Storer, brothers in arms with their pride and joy

Richard Cook of Leeds Rhinos and Laura enjoying Wilsons pies

Say it with a pie!

Russell Walsh at Morecambe FC enjoying a Potts pie with chips and peas

My Growler

'Why growler?' you might ask. Ah well, 'tis so-named because when you bite into this luscious hot meat pie all the lovely jelly gravy oozes out and you just have to growl as you slurp up every last drop!

450 g / 1 lb shortcrust pastry
   (see recipe on page 33)

6 small pie tins or muffin
   moulds, lightly buttered

650 g / 1 lb 6 oz lean British
   beef, minced

Salt and black pepper

Pinch of thyme and crushed
   rosemary

Beef stock

1 egg, beaten with milk, to glaze

Salt and black pepper

Pork stock
   (see recipe on page 48)

MAKES 6

Pre-heat the oven to 200°C / 400°F / gas mark 6.

Prepare the pastry, reserving one third for lids. Roll out on a floured surface to 5 mm / ¼ inch thick and cut out six large circles to fit in the pie tins and six smaller circles for the lids.

Line the tins with the large circles of pastry.

Place the beef into a large bowl and season it well with the herbs, salt and pepper. Add just enough beef stock to moisten the meat and divide it equally into the pie tins.

Cover the tops with the remaining circles of pastry. Make a small hole in the centre of each pie.

Glaze with beaten egg and milk and place the pies onto a baking sheet.

Bake in the centre of the oven for 30–35 minutes until golden brown. Allow to cool slightly and pour the warmed pork stock very carefully into the holes at the top of the pies, until it runs out.

Then get growling ...

Never eat a growler while driving, it gets all over your cockles!

Scouse Pie

Scouse, or 'lobscouse', is a variety of stew that is synonymous with the fine port of Liverpool, though in fact the word comes from the Norwegian 'lapskaus', meaning 'stew'. Versions of Scouse have been popular with sailors throughout northern Europe, and generations of Liverpool workers have come home after a hard day's work to tuck into a big, hearty plate of Scouse before heading off to the pub for a well-deserved pint. My father-in-law, Jim Fitzpatrick, who lived in Bootle, gave this recipe to me. To make the Scouse go further, and for a really filling family pie, you can add pastry, as in this recipe.

BBC Radio presenter Tony Snell bet me I could not get Scouse in a can, so of course I had to take up the challenge! With the help of John Fallon of Grants (famous for canning haggis) I managed to do it, serving it on the Gloria Hunniford Show to Liverpool's very own Gerry Marsden, and sending him away with a can for his mum who was ill in hospital.

900 g / 2 lb neck of mutton, fat and bone removed and cut into cubes then soaked in 600 ml / 1 pint beef stock overnight

450 g / 1 lb stewing steak, cubed and fat removed

50 g / 2 oz dripping

3 large onions, peeled and sliced

900 g / 2 lb potatoes, peeled and diced

2 carrots, peeled and sliced

200 g / 7 oz processed peas

1 teaspoon dried thyme

Salt and black pepper

1 lb shortcrust pastry (see recipe on page 33)

1 egg, beaten, to glaze

SERVES 4–6

Pre-heat the oven to 170ºC / 325ºF / gas mark 3.

Remove the lamb from the beef stock and dry the meat with some kitchen paper towel.

Melt the beef dripping in a deep ovenproof casserole.

Seal the mutton and cubed beef quickly in the hot dripping, add the onions and cook for 6 minutes.

'Lob' all the rest of the ingredients into the casserole, add in the beef stock and just enough water to just cover the ingredients.

Place a lid onto the casserole or cover with cooking foil and cook in the centre of the oven for 3 hours until the scouse is nearly cooked.

Turn the heat up on the oven to 200ºC / 400ºF / gas mark 6.

Top the Scouse with the shortcrust pastry, brush with egg-wash and return to the oven without the lid for a further 35 minutes. Serve with crusty bread.

For 'blind' Scouse, omit the meat and add an extra 900 g / 2 lb of assorted vegetables

The Directors' Box Individual Beef Wellington, or 'Posh Pasty'

I made a beef Wellington at Wembley Stadium in the 1980s and gave one to footballer, pundit and manager Peter Reid, who said I should have been a chef!

One of my favourite chefs and a good friend is Manchester's Robert Owen Brown, owner of the fine eatery The Mark Addy. Robert has won many accolades and with his help we created the following recipe for his team of chefs.

50 g / 2 oz unsalted butter, diced and chilled, plus extra for greasing

2 tablespoons olive oil, for frying

1 large red onion, finely chopped

2 cloves garlic, crushed

225 g / 8 oz wild mushrooms, chopped

1 tablespoons fresh flat leaf parsley, chopped

Salt and black pepper

4 × 200 g / 7 oz fillet steaks, each about 2.5 cm / 1 inch thick

100 g / 4 oz smooth chicken or duck liver pâté

Plain flour, for dusting

1 egg, beaten, to glaze

450 g / 1 lb puff pastry (see recipe on page 39)

SERVES 4–6

Pre-heat the oven to 220°C / 425°F / gas mark 7.

To make the filling, melt half the butter with half the oil in a frying-pan. Add the onion, garlic, and all the mushrooms and sauté for 10 minutes until tender and all the liquid has evaporated. Stir in the parsley, tip into a bowl, season and cool.

Season the steaks. Wipe out the same frying pan and heat until hot, add the remaining oil and sear the seasoned steaks for 1 minute on all sides. Cool, and then spread with pâté.

Cut the pastry into 4 pieces, roll out on a lightly floured surface to 20 cm / 8 inch squares and brush with beaten egg. Divide the mushroom mixture between the squares and place a steak on top, pâté-side down. Bring up two opposite corners of the pastry square to overlap the steak in the centre, seal and gently tuck in the sides, brush with a little beaten egg, and bring the remaining two corners up and seal.

Place the parcels on a heated non-stick baking sheet, brush with beaten egg and bake in the oven for 20 minutes.

It is important that the steaks be rare for that added flavour

Wiganer's Delight

I created these pies for my chief pie tasters Ernie and Sandra Clark, who are real Wiganers!

25 g / 1 oz beef dripping

1 kg / 2¼ lb lean minced beef

450 g / 1 lb potatoes, peeled and diced

225 g / 8 oz chopped red onion

1 tablespoon mixed herbs

25 g / 1 oz plain flour

300 ml / 10 fl oz beef stock

1 teaspoon Worcestershire sauce

Salt and black pepper

225 g / 8 oz real Lancashire black pudding, skin removed and diced

450 g / 1 lb shortcrust pastry (see recipe on page 33)

450 g / 1 lb puff pastry (see recipe on page 39)

1 egg, beaten, to glaze

MAKES 6

Pre-heat the oven to 200°C / 400°F / gas mark 6.

In a large saucepan heat the dripping until it is quite hot, add the mince and very quickly seal and brown it for 3 minutes. Add the potatoes, onion and mixed herbs, cooking for 2 minutes, then sprinkle with the flour and stir.

Add the beef stock and Worcestershire sauce and bring to the boil slowly, simmering for 20 minutes. Season well and taste. Carefully remove about 120 ml / 4 fl oz of the stock from the minced beef (you can use this to make pouring gravy).

Prepare the pastry and set aside one-third for the lids.

Roll out the pastry on a floured surface to 5 mm / ¼ inch thick. Cut out six large circles to fit in the pie tins and line the tins.

Divide the mince filling equally into the pie tins and sprinkle with the diced black pudding.

Roll out the puff pastry and cover the pie dishes, sealing and crimping the pastry all around.

Trim off any excess pastry and use to decorate and then glaze.

Bake in the centre of the oven for 40–45 minutes.

The **Great North Pie** Company

I met Neil and Vicki Broomfield, who set up the Great North Pie Company, at Nigel Haworth's fantastic food show in Ewood Park Football Stadium, Blackburn. They are true artisan pie-makers, happy and proud to keep everything on a small scale and with no plans for world domination! Only a small number of pies are made each week, all of which are individually hand finished and use only the best local and seasonal ingredients, which enables them to maintain their incredibly high quality standards.

Based in Cheshire and working from a small kitchen, Great North's mouth-watering pies change every month. One special is *Potted Shrimp and Butter Pie*, made with Morecambe bay shrimps, white onion, lemon, potato, cream, cayenne, white pepper, nutmeg and mace. Another is *Cheshire Cheese, Leek and Apple*, which as a cheese-lover I was bowled over by. The filling for this was Joseph Heler's Cheshire Blue cheese, Granny Smith and Bramley apples, leeks, thyme and spiced walnut breadcrumbs. Inventive or wot – pure pie genius! And it's not just me who thinks so; the special pies the company produces have earned numerous accolades, including Reserve Champion in the Fish Pie section (for the Shrimp Pie) at the British Pie Awards 2010, a 3-star Gold in the Great Taste Awards in 2009, and Cheshire Life Food Hero in 2008, to name just a few.

You can contact them at info@thegreatnorthpiecompany.co.uk, and look out for their website at www.thegreatnorthpiecompany.co.uk.

Goddard's Pie & Mash Shop

Pie 'n' mash is one of the oldest regional dishes that London has to offer. Forget your chip shops and burger bars, 'Pie 'n' Mash Houses' have been around since the early 1800s, and there has been a great revival recently in these dishes, with quite a number of 'pie 'n' mash' restaurants now to be found across London.

One of the oldest pie producers in the area is Goddard's, who opened their doors in 1890 in Evelyn Street, Deptford. As a pie-maker by the Thames, in the early days they inevitably specialised in fish-based versions such as eel pie, although they also offered pies filled with beef and vegetables under a pastry crust. Traditionally, these pies were served with a healthy dollop of mash, covered in parsley gravy or 'liquor'.

The descendants of the founder, Alfred Goddard, still own and run the company, and are as passionately dedicated as he was to making traditional pie, mash and liquor, so all of the pies are still hand-made and hand-assembled, as has been the case for generations. You can buy their wares on weekends and bank holidays from their booth in Fountain Court on Greenwich Church Street, but the major part of their business these days is producing in much larger quantities for trade and online orders. Which is excellent news if you don't live in London!

For further information and to order their wonderful pies and mash online, visit www.pieshop.co.uk.

Lamb Patties

This recipe dates back to 1813, and is from the *Frugal Housewife* cookbook, one of those in my collection of old recipe books.

300 g / 12 oz shortcrust pastry
(see recipe on page 33)

450 g / 1 lb cold mutton or lamb

2 Cox's Orange Pippin apples,
peeled, cored and chopped

6 prunes, stoned and chopped

1 pinch of nutmeg

1 pinch of salt

2 tablespoons port

Redcurrant jelly

1 egg, beaten, to glaze

MAKES 6

Roll out the pastry and line patty tins, reserving enough for lids.

Cut the cold meat into small pieces and combine the meat and apples with the prunes, nutmeg and salt. Moisten with the port.

Put a large spoonful of meat mixture in the centre of each little pie.

Cover with pastry lids, cut a hole in the top of each pie, and glaze.

Bake at 220ºC / 425ºF / gas mark 7 at the top of the oven for 20 minutes.

Melt the redcurrant jelly by warming it in a pan and pour a little into every pie through the hole in the top.

Allow to cool and eat cold.

A Merry Meaty Christmas Slice

On a wonderful sunny Wednesday afternoon in March 2010 I hosted the Wigan Food Festival, at which my special guest was Antony Worrall Thompson. Having worked with Antony on several occasions, I just knew the afternoon would be great fun, and it was! The day was aimed at using leftover food to support the Love Food Hate Waste campaign and Antony made a roast lamb salad on a potato cake, which was a big hit with the very appreciative audience.

I am equally passionate about wasting nothing, and one of my favourite recipes is a festive one I make every year for my family. My Christmas meat slice is basically made up of leftover meats, with added extras, lined with stuffing, and it is nice hot or cold. Use whatever meat is left over and layer each between some stuffing for a marbled effect when you cut into it.

450 g / 1 lb shortcrust cheese pastry (see recipe on page 41)

15 ml / 1 tablespoon English mustard powder

1 black pudding ring, skin removed

100 g / 4 oz cooked pork leg, or leftover pork

100 g / 4 oz cooked silverside of beef, or leftover beef

100 g / 4 oz cooked chicken meat or leftover chicken

200 g / 7 oz apricot and cranberry stuffing (see recipe on page 249)

3 tablespoons chicken stock

Salt and black pepper

1 egg, beaten to seal and glaze

SERVES 4–6

Pre-heat the oven to 200°C / 400°F / gas mark 6.

Roll out the pastry and make it into an oblong shape, like you would for an extra large sausage roll!

Place the pastry onto a large, lightly greased baking tray.

Brush along the centre of the pastry with the English mustard and line the centre first with the black pudding, then add a little stock and place thin slices of stuffing on top.

Place pork meat on next, season and repeat this process, using the chicken and beef. Egg-wash along the front and back of the oblong pastry. Carefully bring the pastry over the meat, like you would a sausage roll. Pressing the edges together, then turning over, ensuring that the join is underneath the meat roll.

Brush the pastry with the beaten egg and bake in the centre of the oven for 20–25 minutes. Allow to cool and serve with piccalilli.

Beef Korma Curry Pies

Curries, which of course originated in the Far East, have become very popular throughout the world. They vary hugely between countries and within countries, so that Malaysian and Vietnamese curries are poles apart, and in India, for example, a dish from the Kerala region is very different from one that is typical of Goa or the Punjab.

And curry need not be the hot and fiery things we so often get in this country, where the average cook seems to cherish the idea that the hotter the curry the more genuine it is. Traditional curries are much more subtle than that, and Madhur Jaffrey once told me that it is not hard to master Indian spices as long as you don't have a clumsy hand.

As a food historian I couldn't resist this recipe from 1865, which I have converted for the twentieth century:

50 g / 2 oz butter

3 onions, sliced

30 ml / 2 tablespoons of ground shallots

5 ml / 1 teaspoon coriander seed

3 cloves of garlic

5 ml / 1 teaspoon ground chillies

5 ml / 1 teaspoon ground turmeric and ground ginger

6 ground cardamoms

2 cloves

2 sticks of ground cinnamon

Pinch of saffron

450 g / 1 lb of cubed rump steak

150 ml / ¼ pint of beef stock

150 ml / ¼ pint dahi (curd) or sour cream *

Juice of 2 lemons

450 g / 1 lb shortcrust pastry
(see recipe on page 33)

1 egg, beaten, to glaze

MAKES 6

---

* Dahi (curds). These curds are made by milk being brought to the boil and while it is still warm adding a little vinegar or tartaric acid, then allowing to stand for 12 hours. It turns into a thick cream. which can be used in curries, although in India it is also served as a sweet with sugar, or eaten with salt and rice.

In a large casserole melt the butter and sauté the sliced onions, shallots and garlic until they are brown. Then add all the herbs and spices, stir well and sizzle for 3 minutes.

Place the meat in the casserole and brown for 5 minutes.

Add the beef stock and cook at 180°C / 350°F / gas mark 4 for 45 minutes.

Add the dahi or sour cream and lemon juice, fold in very carefully and cook for a further 15 minutes. Allow the mixture to cool, pour through a colander, reserve the sauce and use the filling for the pies.

Re-set the oven to 200°C / 400°F / gas mark 6.

Prepare the shortcrust pastry, set aside a third for the lids.

Roll out the pastry on a floured surface to 5 mm / ¼ inch thick. Cut out six large circles to fit in the pie tins. Line the tins with the pastry.

Divide the korma filling equally into the pie tins. Roll out the remaining pastry and cover the pie dishes, sealing and crimping the pastry all around.

Trim of any excess pastry and decorate with pastry leaves and glaze.

Bake in the centre of the oven for 40 to 45 minutes.

Shirley Roberts' Rich Steak & Red Wine Pies

Shirley's Handmade Pies really are extra special, and she prides herself on using only the finest ingredients. This is my recipe, which Shirley has approved.

25 g / 1 oz lard

675 g / 1½ lb chuck steak, cut into chunks, fat removed

2 onions, finely chopped

40 g /1½ oz plain flour

½ teaspoon nutmeg grated

425 ml / 15 fl oz rich beef stock

75 ml / 3 fl oz full bodied red wine

Salt and black pepper

1 tablespoon chopped parsley

1 teaspoon lemon juice

1 lb shortcrust pastry (see recipe on page 33)

1 egg, beaten, to glaze

MAKES 6

In a large non-stick saucepan heat the lard and fry the steak for 4 minutes. Add the onions and cook for a further 2 minutes. Sprinkle with flour and nutmeg and cook for 3 minutes, adding the beef stock, red wine, seasoning, parsley and lemon juice, and simmering for 60 minutes. Allow the beef mixture to cool completely.

Roll out the pastry on a floured surface to 5 mm / ¼ inch thick. Cut out six large circles to fit in the pie tins and six smaller circles for the lids. Line the tins with the large circles of pastry.

Place the beef mixture onto the pastry and top off with the pastry lids. Glaze with beaten egg and place the pies onto a baking sheet. Bake in a pre-heated oven to 200°C / 400°F / gas mark 6 for 35 minutes.

Cheese, Potato & Onion Pies

These pies, based on a Shirley Roberts recipe, taste as good as they look. I made a mini version using Red Leicester cheese for a truly wonderful young lady called Becky Want who works for the BBC. She had just completed the London Marathon and raised a massive amount of money for Christie's Hospital and she was vowing 'Never again!', but I reckon after one of my mini cheese pies anyone'd have enough energy to run for miles!

1 large potato, peeled and cut into cubes

2 onions, finely sliced

1 tablespoon plain flour

50 ml / 2 oz whole milk

50 ml / 2 oz double cream

150 g / 5 oz mature Cheddar cheese, grated

½ teaspoon English mustard powder

½ teaspoon cayenne pepper

Salt and black pepper

1 lb shortcrust pastry (see recipe on page 33)

1 egg, beaten, to glaze

MAKES 6

Bring a saucepan of salted water to the boil. Add the potato pieces to the pan and cook for 10–15 minutes, or until tender, then drain well and set aside.

In a separate saucepan boil 425 ml / 15 fl oz water, add the sliced onions and cook for 2–3 minutes, or until softened. Drain well and return the cooked onions to the saucepan.

Sprinkle the onions with the flour and stir well to coat. Add the milk and cream and heat the mixture over a medium heat for 3 minutes, stirring continuously.

Add the cooked potato pieces, grated cheese, mustard and cayenne pepper and stir well. Season to taste with salt and pepper, stir well and set aside to cool.

Pre-heat the oven to 180°C / 350°F / gas mark 4.

Prepare the pastry, set aside one-third for the lids.

Roll out the pastry on a floured surface to 5 mm / ¼ inch thick. Cut out six large circles to fit in the pie tins and six smaller circles for the lids. Line the tins with the large circles of pastry.

Divide the cheese and onion filling equally into the pie tins. Cover each pie with the remaining circles of pastry and make a small hole in the centre of each pie.

Glaze with beaten egg and place the pies onto a baking sheet.

Bake for 35 minutes in the centre of the oven.

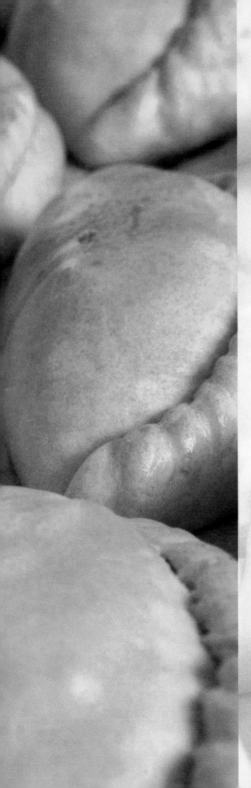

The pasty

One of the earliest references to a pasty is from the late twelfth century in connection with one of King Arthur's knights, while Robin Hood sings of pasties in his ballads in the 1300s: 'Bred in chese, butre an milk, pastees and flaunes.' King Henry VIII's wife, Jane Seymour, was also known to enjoy her pasties in the sixteenth century, and even Shakespeare makes a reference to them, in the *Merry Wives of Windsor* in 1600: 'Come, we have a hot pasty to dinner.'

A pasty is different from a pie because it is made by placing the filling on a flat pastry shape, usually round, rather than in a dish or tin, and then folding it to wrap the filling, crimping the edge to form a seal. The result is a hearty package with a crimped edge that is sometimes along the top, sometimes along one edge.

There are so many varieties of pasty made in the UK and I would love to include them all here, but my publisher says I can't! What you will find here, though, is a mouthwatering selection of regional versions, together with some of my own favourites.

Eighteenth-century Cornish Pasty

I have adapted this from the original, which is remarkably similar to the recipes used today by authentic Cornish pasty makers.

Shortcrust pastry

225 g / 8 oz plain flour

115 g / 4½ oz fat (mixture of lard and butter)

Pinch of salt

Filling

4 large potatoes, thinly sliced

1 large swede, thinly sliced

450 g / 1 lb steak cut into small cubes

2 onions, peeled and chopped

Salt and pepper

1 egg, beaten, to glaze

MAKES 4

Make up the shortcrust pastry, for guidance see the recipe on page 33.

Roll out the pastry into 4 rounds using a large saucer as a guide, about 5 mm / ¼ inch thick.

Place a layer of the potatoes thinly onto the centre of each round to form a base for the rest of the filling. Add the swede thinly over the potato, then spread the steak on top. Add a little onion, season with salt and pepper.

Dampen the edge of the circle of pastry with water to help seal it, bring together the edges to make a parcel with the filling in the centre. There should be a neat pastry parcel but if you do get any holes, patch them with a little extra pastry. You can make the pastry neater by crimping the edges: fold over the edge to make it slightly thicker, and then squeeze tightly every 2 cm / 1 inch to make a neat pattern along the edge.

Put the pasties on a piece of buttered paper, make a small slit on the top to let the steam out, and glaze.

Put the pasties on a greased baking tray and bake in a pre-heated oven at 200°C / 400°F / gas mark 6 for 30 minutes, then reduce the heat to 190°C / 375°F / gas mark 5 and cook for another 30 minutes.

The legendary Cornish pasty

Cornish pasties have existed for at least 300 years, probably longer. It is difficult to know exactly when and why they were invented, but over the centuries they became a portable lunchtime meal for Cornish miners, engineers, blacksmiths, farm labourers etc. Interestingly, although fishermen too enjoyed their pasties they believed that they would bring bad luck at sea – so much so that even partially eaten ones were left ashore!

Wives would carve their husbands' initials in the corner of each pasty so that when, as was common, half was eaten for breakfast and the rest saved for lunch, they would know which belonged to whom. And the reason that a traditional Cornish pasty has a substantial crimp on the side (rather than along the top which is characteristic of a Devon pasty) is so that a miner or other manual labourer with dirty hands could eat his lunch then throw away the bit he'd contaminated by holding it. The pastry of pasties past must been very substantial, too, because apparently it could stay warm for 8 to 10 hours and, when carried close to the body, could help keep its owner warm.

Nowadays, the Cornish pasty is enjoyed the country – and indeed, the world – over, although there is a fierce debate about which pasties may be called Cornish. Local producers feel strongly that only pasties made in the county of origin, to a traditional recipe and manner, can legally be called 'Cornish' pasties.

Visit www.cornishpastyassociation.co.uk for loads more fascinating stuff on this legendary regional food hero.

Ann's Pasties: 'a dream folded in heaven'

I have several food heroes in this business, like Shirley Roberts, Marie Walsh, Richard Earl of Bradford, haggis man John Fallon and Wilsons of Yorkshire. And when it comes to the iconic Cornish pasty the best maker in Cornwall has to be Ann Muller, owner of Ann's Pies:

> You never talk of a 'Cornish pasty' in Cornwall. It's always pasty, pure and simple. The second most important thing to remember when considering this savoury parcel is that a proper pasty is a meal in itself. Putting it on a plate with chips is ignorant and a sure sign that the kitchen from where it emerged spared little regard for the quality of the pasty itself. Third, it is important to note that the filling always goes into the pasty raw.
>
> I never expected to become a Cornish pasty-maker. My only previous catering experience was waitressing in a vegetarian restaurant in Notting Hill, West London, over 30 years ago, to help me through art school. I'd never even made a pasty until about 20 years ago, even though it's something, which all the women in my mother's Cornish family traditionally did.
>
> I learnt in an emergency, I was summoned by my mother, Hettie Merrick, a professional pasty-maker, to a Breton agricultural fair, where demand was dramatically and unexpectedly outstripping supply at a stall mother had set up. At the end of a day of pasty-making, I could crimp them as fast as my mother, which was the perfect confidence boost and eye opener into the fact that there was a business to be had producing a good Cornish pasty.

A very good business is exactly what Ann now has, still making pasties by hand, and, as her mother proudly says of her daughter's wares, 'Every mouthful is a piece of Cornwall – a dream folded in heaven.'

See www.annspasties.co.uk for more information.

Florence's Cornish Pasty

This recipe is taken from Florence White's *Good Things in England*, of 1922. I did make pasties from this recipe and they were lovely, but I must admit that I wasn't too keen on the calf's liver. You can try it with and without if you like, or just enjoy the recipe as an curiosity!

Pastry

450 g / ½ lb flour

75 g / 3 oz lard or dripping

Pinch of salt

60 ml / 2½ fl oz water to make a
   fine dough

Filling

225 g / 8 oz beef steak

100 g / 4 oz calf's liver

2 potatoes

1 large onion

1 medium turnip

1 large carrot

Salt and pepper

Egg white, to glaze

SERVES 4–6

Pre-heat the oven to 180ºC / 350ºF / gas mark 4.

Roll out the dough fairly thin, cut into 4–6 squares.

Chop the steak and liver finely, mix together and season.

Peel, or scrape, and slice the potatoes, onion, turnip and carrot.

Mix and season the vegetables.

Put a layer of vegetables on half of each square of pastry and some of the chopped meat on top.

Brush the edges of the pastry with white of egg, fold the plain half over the meat and Pinch the edges well together.

N.B. It is important to close the edges neatly and closely, so that no steam escapes, and to use uncooked meat and vegetables. The contents cook in their own juices, so after the first few minutes require a very moderate oven. The above amounts make 2 large or 3 medium-sized pasties.

Bake for 45 minutes or just until pastry is golden.

Chicken Masala Pasties

Indian restaurateur Ramon Kapur gave me this recipe, and what a beauty it is! If you can, use thigh meat; it has a far better taste than breast meat and also has the advantage of being cheaper. I make the pasty like I would one my jumbo Eccles cakes, as a fat circular patty.

60 ml / 4 tablespoons sunflower oil

2 large red onions thinly sliced

1 large beef tomato diced

2 tablespoons garlic paste

1 tablespoon ginger paste

2 teaspoons coriander powder

1 teaspoon cumin powder

½ teaspoon turmeric powder

½ teaspoon red chilli powder

3 teaspoons garam masala powder

1 large green pepper chopped

1 kg / 2¼ lb boneless chicken pieces, skin removed

100 ml / 4 fl oz chicken stock

100 ml / 4 fl oz soured cream

Salt and black pepper

450 g / 1 lb shortcrust pastry (see recipe on page 33)

1 egg, beaten, to glaze

Heat the oil in a pan and fry the onions until golden brown. Remove onions from the oil with a slotted spoon and drain on kitchen paper towels.

Blend the onions into a smooth paste in a food processor and remove into a separate container.

Now blend the tomatoes, garlic and ginger pastes together into one smooth paste.

Heat the remaining oil and add the onion paste. Fry for 3 minutes.

Add the tomato paste and all the spices. Mix to form the masala.

Fry the masala until the oil begins to separate from it then add the green pepper and chicken and brown well.

Slowly add the chicken stock and soured cream to the pan, simmer and cover. Cook for 5 minutes and place to one side.

Roll out the pastry to about 5 mm / ¼ inch thick and cut into 30 cm circles.

Place a small tablespoonful of filling into the centre of each circle. Draw the edges together over the chicken and pinch to seal. Turn over and press gently to flatten the pasties. You can use small, shallow tins instead if you wish.

Make a small slash in the top of each pasty, place on a baking tray and glaze.

Bake in the centre of the oven for about 30 minutes at 220ºC / 425ºF / gas mark 6.

Ginsters

Everyone knows the name Ginsters; they really are a huge pie-making outfit. What most people don't know, though, is that they started life as a small, family-run egg-packing business, of all things. Then, one Christmas, the family hit upon a great idea that changed the course of history – well, theirs anyway! They converted their egg-packing plant into a small bakery and started making delicious, authentic Cornish pasties.

Back then, just 30 people worked at the Ginsters bakery, whereas today over 700 people produce over three million pastries, using the freshest ingredients from local suppliers, and the original recipe. Of course, they've had to build a bigger bakery to achieve this … it'd be a bit cramped otherwise! Since 1977, the company has been a part of Samworth Brothers Ltd and now has a huge range of pies, rolls, pasties, sandwiches and wraps. It is Ginsters Original Cornish Pasty, however, that is the nation's biggest selling product in the chilled savouries market. Not bad for humble egg-packers!

The Ultimate Cheese & Onion Pasty

I love cheese and I have tried a variety of cheese pasties throughout the UK. But when making a cheese pasty the mix must be just right; it must be more cheese than potato, the onions should be fried in butter, and a Cheddar cheese pastry should be used to complement it. And I agree with Ann Muller: like her Cornish pasty, this should not be served with chips or vegetables or beans. It is to be enjoyed on its own.

450 g / 1 lb Cheddar cheese pastry (see recipe on page 41)

350 g / 12 oz new potatoes, peeled, diced and cooked until tender

225 g / 8 oz crumbly Lancashire cheese, broken up

225 g / 8 oz mature Cheddar, grated

1 teaspoon English mustard powder

2 egg yolks

60 ml double cream

2 red onions, thinly sliced and fried in 50 g / 2 oz butter until soft

Salt and black pepper

1 egg, beaten, to glaze

MAKES 6

Pre-heat the oven to 200°C / 400°F / gas mark 6.

Make up the Cheddar cheese pastry and let it rest for 20 minutes.

Meanwhile for the filling, place the potatoes, cheeses, mustard, egg yolks, cream and red onions into a bowl. Season with salt and pepper and mix well.

Roll out the pastry into 6 rounds using a large saucer as a guide, about 5 mm / ¼ inch thick.

Place the potato mixture onto one half of the pastry. Fold over the other half to cover, crimp the edges to seal and glaze. Place onto a baking sheet and put in the oven to bake for 25 minutes, or until crisp and golden.

Try adding some York ham or naturally cured streaky bacon cooked until crisp

Meg Dod's Venison Pasty

Meg Dod, christened Isobel Christian Johnston, was one of the greatest Scottish cooks and the author of *The Cook and Housewife's Manual* in 1826. Just for interest, I've included her original recipe at the bottom of the page below my updated version. You will notice that in Meg's recipe it is not a pasty in the way that we would think of one – instead of the characteristic moon-shaped parcel this is really a pie with only a pastry lid.

Meg's venison pasty for the twenty-first-century cook

675 g / 1½ lb loin of venison

50 g / 2 oz butter

15 ml / 1 tablespoon cooking oil

1 red onion, finely chopped

30 ml / 2 tablespoons flour

300 ml / ½ pint game stock

½ teaspoon mace

½ teaspoon allspice

150 ml / ¼ pint of claret

2 tablespoons shallot vinegar
   (you can buy this or make it
   by soaking finely chopped
   shallots in red wine vinegar
   for a few days)

2 tablespoons rowan jelly

Salt and black pepper

1 lb hot water pastry
   (see recipe on page 36)

1 egg, beaten, to glaze

MAKES 6

Cut the venison into 5 cm / 2 inch cubes, trimming away any tough membrane or sinew. Heat the butter and oil in a large saucepan, add the venison and onion and brown the meat, cooking for about 4 minutes.

Sprinkle on the flour and cook for a further 3 minutes. Now add the game stock and cook out for 10 minutes, slowly adding the rest of the ingredients, blending thoroughly and simmering for 30 minutes.

Pre-heat the oven to 180°C / 350°F / gas mark 4.

Allow the venison filling to cool slightly, pour into a deep pie dish and top with the pastry, decorating with leaf shapes in a circle and glaze. Bake in the oven for 80 minutes.

Allow the pasty to rest for 5 minutes before serving with some minted new potatoes and warm Red Velvet beetroot.

Venison, gravy, pepper, salt, mace, allspice, claret or port, eschalot vinegar, onions (optional) and pastry.

*A modern pasty is made of what does not roast well, as the neck, the breast, the shoulder. The breast makes a good pasty. Cut into little chops, trimmings off all bones and skins. Make some good **gravy from the bones** and other trimmings. Place fat and lean pieces of meat together, or, if very lean, place thin slices from the firm fat of a leg or a neck of mutton along with each piece.*

*Season the meat with **pepper, salt**, pounded mace, and allspice. Place it handsomely in a dish and put in the drawn gravy, a quarter-pint of claret or port, a glassful of eschalot vinegar, and, if liked, a couple of onions very finely shred. Cover the dish with a **thick crust**.*

Priddy Oggies

This lovely pasty from the village of Priddy in Somerset is made using their local pork and Cheddar, making this is a true regional speciality.

350 g / 12 oz Gloucester Old
 Spot pork fillet

6 thin naturally cured smoked
 bacon rashers

175 g / 6 oz grated Cheddar
 cheese

1 teaspoon chopped parsley

Salt and black pepper

1 egg, beaten, to glaze

1 lb Cheddar cheese pastry
 (see recipe on page 41)

1 egg, beaten, to glaze

MAKES 6

Slice the pork fillet lengthwise almost through, and with some cling film cover the pork and beat it very thin with a rolling pin, or meat mallet.

Remove the cling film and lay on the bacon to cover the pork.

Mix the Cheddar cheese, parsley, seasoning and beaten egg together and spread the mixture over the bacon.

Carefully roll up the pork fillet into a long Swiss roll shape. Wrap this in damp greaseproof paper and refrigerate for 1 hour.

Pre-heat the oven to 180°C / 350°F / gas mark 4.

Roll the pastry out into an oblong and cut into 6 pieces 15 × 7.5 cm / 6 × 3 inch.

Cut the pork into 4 cm / 1½ inch long pieces and place one on each piece of pastry.

Fold the pastry over the pork, pressing the edges together, and glaze.

Bake in the centre of the oven for 30 minutes until crisp and serve with a light salad and a glass of cider.

Oggie is the West Country word for pasty

The Bordi Calzone

One of my favourite restaurants is Casa Italia in Liverpool, which is run by the Bordi family and Dave Cross, who is a genius when it comes to attention to detail. I have included the Bordi basic calzone filling as an alternative to my cacciatore.

The Bordi basic calzone filling

175 g / 6 oz finely sliced cooked
    quality ham, shredded

175 g / 6 oz mozzarella, diced

8 fresh basil leaves, torn

6 Italian vine tomatoes, peeled,
    seeded and diced

60 ml / 4 tablespoons freshly
    grated Parmesan cheese

Salt and black pepper

1 lb calzone dough
    (see recipe on page 43)

A little olive oil

MAKES 4

Combine all the filling ingredients in a bowl and put to one side.

Punch the calzone dough down and knead it lightly on a floured board, divide into 4 and roll into balls.

Roll each ball into a flat circle about 5 mm / ¼ inch in thickness

Divide the filling between the four circles of dough, placing it onto half of each circle; allow a border of 2 cm / 1 inch.

Fold the other half of the dough circle over and crimp the edges together with your fingers and seal like you would a Cornish pasty.

Place the calzone onto the baking sheets, brush lightly with olive oil and bake in the centre of the oven for 15–20 minutes.

Serve with a light salad.

I like to add pepperoni to mine

Cacciatore Pasty, or Casa Italia Calzone

This is something completely different that I developed around 1983 for Warburtons. I make the cacciatore filling the day before I make this pasty, allowing the flavours of the chicken to infuse. I dedicate this to Sharon and Dave Cross!

60 ml / 4 tablespoons olive oil

50 g / 2 oz butter

4 garlic cloves crushed

1.35 kg / 3 lb chicken meat off the bone, skin removed

16 shallots peeled

350 g / 12 oz wild mushrooms, chopped

1 kg / 2¼ lb Italian tomatoes, chopped

300 ml / ½ pint red wine

60 ml / 4 tablespoons tomato puree

1 teaspoon chopped rosemary

1 sprig of fresh rosemary

Salt and black pepper

1 kg / 2¼ lb ready-made shortcrust or calzone pastry (see recipe on page 43)

170 g / 6 oz pepperoni sausage, sliced

160 g / 6 oz grated Cheddar cheese

1 large egg, beaten with 30 ml / 2 tablespoons of fresh milk, to glaze

Heat the oil and butter in a large flameproof casserole until hot. Add the garlic and chicken and sauté over a medium heat for 6 minutes.

Add the shallots and mushrooms, cook for 4 minutes, stirring frequently. Add the rest of the ingredients, seasoning well.

Gently bring to the boil and simmer for 45 minutes, stirring every 15 minutes.

Remove the rosemary stalk from the casserole and let the cacciatore filling stand for at least 1 hour to allow it to cool completely.

Pre-heat the oven to 220°C / 425°F / gas mark 7.

Flour a work surface and roll out the pastry to about 5 mm / ¼ inch thick and cut out four to six 15 cm / 6 inch rounds.

Put 110 g / 4 oz cacciatore mixture into the centre of each round, top with 4 slices of pepperoni and 25 g / 1 oz grated cheese.

Dampen the edge of the rounds with beaten egg mixture; fold each round over to make a half moon shape.

Turn the edges round to make, small turns (horns), pinching and crimping the edges to seal the pasty completely. Glaze with beaten egg and place the pasties onto a greased baking sheet.

Bake the centre of the oven, lowering the heat after 10 minutes to 180°C / 350°F / gas mark 4, for a total of 30 minutes.

MAKES APPROX 12 PASTIES

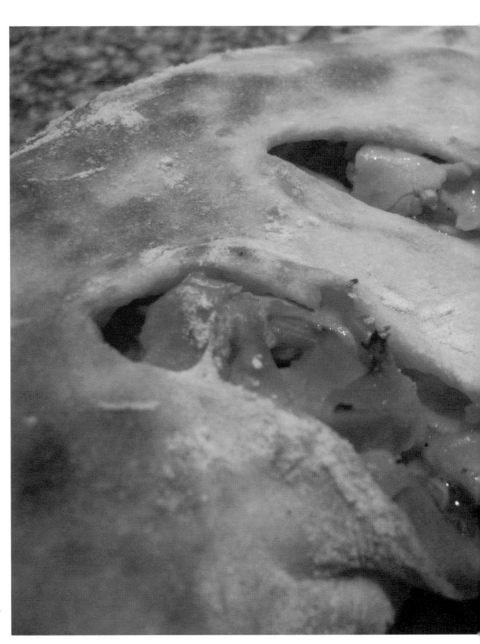

This shows the deep fried Calzone from Domenico Crolla, owner of Bella Napoli in Glasgow

Nutter's 'Up the Dale' Pie

It was 2007, centenary year for Rochdale FC, and as it happened the team reached the play-offs for the 1st division. So to celebrate this occasion I created a pie not just for the team but for the supporters as well – it went down a storm and even featured on Sky TV! I'm dedicating this recipe to Andrew Nutter, one of the greatest chefs in this industry and a young man with old school disciplines and one of the nicest people you could ever meet. We worked together in May 2010 for the Southport Food Festival and he is one of the most entertaining of the new breed of celebrity chefs, with masses of culinary quirks. His restaurant in Rochdale, Nutters, is well worth a visit.

You don't have to be a nutter to make this dish, of course, and you don't have to be a nutter to support Rochdale FC … actually, on second thoughts, maybe you do!

4 shortcrust pastry tarts lined in pie tins and baked blind

1 cooked Désirée potato, crushed

1 tablespoon olive oil

1 small leek, finely chopped

1 clove garlic

2 rashers streaky bacon, cooked and chopped

Few splashes Worcestershire sauce

1 poached chicken breast, cut into thin strips

1 black pudding, cut into thin strips

SERVES 4

Take the crushed potato and use to fill each pie case three-quarters full.

Heat the olive oil and fry the leeks and garlic together for two minutes until softened – mix in the chopped bacon and spoon on top of the potato.

Splash some Worcestershire sauce over each pie and top with alternate strips of black pudding and chicken and season.

Serve cold or warm through in an oven with a generous spoonful of proper gravy.

Forfar Bridies

Allegedly these were invented by Mr Jolly, a baker in Forfar, around the 1870s. Why bridies? Well, some say it's because they are a simple meal that a young bride could add to her cookery book, while other stories hold that they were made for wedding meals (the brides' meal), hence the traditional horseshoe shape for luck. Another story is that they were made by Margaret Bridie from Glamis, who sold them at the Buttermarket in Forfar.

450 g / 1 lb shortcrust pastry (see recipe on page 33)

75 g / 3 oz beef suet

450 g / 1 lb rump steak, diced

2 onions, finely chopped

Salt and black pepper

1 tablespoon parsley

1 egg, beaten with a little milk, to glaze

MAKES 6

Pre-heat the oven to 200°C / 400°F / gas mark 6.

Roll out the pastry to about 5 mm / ¼ inch thick and cut out four to six 15 cm / 6 inch rounds.

Place the beef, suet and chopped onions into a bowl and season well, mixing all the ingredients together.

Put equal amounts of the mixture into the centre of each round.

Dampen the edge of the rounds with beaten egg; fold each round over to make a half-moon shape.

Turn the edges round to make small turns (horns), pinching and crimping the edges to seal the pasty completely. Glaze with beaten egg and place the bridies onto a greased baking sheet.

Bake the centre of the oven, lowering the heat after 10 minutes to 180°C / 350°F / gas mark 4, for 45 minutes.

Bolton-based Carrs Pasties

In 1939, with war clouds looming, Joe and Nelly Carr moved into Nelly's mother's UCP tripe shop on Halliwell Road, Bolton. The only things sold there were tripe, cowheels, trotters, Smiths potato crisps (including the small blue bag of salt) and refillable soda-water siphon bottles. When war broke out Joe Carr worked in a munitions factory, while Nelly looked after the tripe shop and her children. During this time, while baking for the family, Nelly decided to introduce fruit pies and plain cakes to sell.

As the family grew, they decided to move into a house a short distance away and began to introduce pies and pasties to the stock-in-trade. Ater the war, when rationing was lifted, demand increased so production moved up a gear. Joe and Nelly now began working full-time in the shop, pasties became the most popular line, the 'tripe shop' became known as the 'pastie shop', and the trade name 'Carrs Pasties' was adopted.

These days Carrs make over 6,000 fresh products every day and up to 40,000 products per week, the majority being pasties, using locally sourced ingredients wherever possible.

The 'Bowton' Meat & Potato Pasty

One of the North West's most prized food outlets is Ye Olde Pastie Shoppe in Bolton, established in 1667. It's only open on weekdays, when you will find a big queue for the pasties and whist pies which are prepared under the watchful eye of owner Marie Walsh. The list of the great and good who have passed through its hallowed doors is very long, and includes the likes of Nat Lofthouse, Freddie Flintoff and our local comedy pride and joy, Peter Kay. My mother had a pub called the Gypsies Tent in Manchester over 35 years ago and she would buy a tray of Marie's pasties on a daily basis for the pub regulars, who enjoyed them with a good pint.

I'm afraid that this is only my version of this pasty because the recipe for the original one is a closely guarded secret! What I can do, though, is help you re-create, step by step, the folding of this famous pasty and to give you a pretty tasty filling.

25 g / 1 oz beef dripping

450 g / 1 lb of lean minced beef

1 kg /2¼ lb King Edward
    potatoes, peeled and diced

225 g / 8 oz chopped red onion

1 tablespoon mixed herbs

25 g / 1 oz plain flour

300 ml / 10 fl oz beef stock

1 teaspoon Worcestershire
    sauce

Salt and black pepper

1 lb shortcrust pastry
    (see recipe on page 33)

A little milk

MAKES 6

In a large saucepan heat the dripping until it is quite hot, add the mince and very quickly seal and brown it for 3 minutes. Add the potatoes, onion and mixed herbs, cooking for 2 minutes, then sprinkle with the flour and stir in the beef stock and Worcestershire sauce. Bring to the boil slowly and let it simmer for 20 minutes. Season well and taste.

Carefully remove about 120 ml / 4½ fl oz of the gravy from the minced beef and retain.

Roll out the pastry into 6 rounds about 5 mm / ¼ inch thick. Dampen the edge of the circle of pastry with water to help seal it, place in your filling and half fold over to a half moon shape. Then fold over the front, back to the centre of the pasty bring together the edges make a parcel with the filling in the centre.

There should be a neat pastry parcel. If you do get any holes, then patch them with a little and final fold in the edge on both sides and then squeeze tightly.

Put each pasty on a piece of buttered paper, brush the tops with a little milk and lay on a greased baking tray.

Bake in a pre-heated oven at 200ºC / 400ºF / gas mark 6 for 25 minutes.

Purple Sprouting Broccoli & Stilton Pasties

I just love purple sprouting broccoli with a good, creamy Stilton, so putting the two together inside a pastry jacket has got to be a winner – it's just a shame really that the lovely purple turns to green when it is cooked!

2 tablespoons olive oil

2 red onions, peeled and sliced

225 g / 8 oz purple sprouting broccoli

450 g / 1 lb puff pastry (see recipe on page 39)

275 g / 10 oz Stilton cheese

225 g / 8 oz mashed potato

Salt and black pepper

1 egg yolk blended with 5 ml / 1 teaspoon of fresh milk, to glaze

MAKES 6

Always use fresh broccoli and not frozen!

Pre-heat oven to 220ºC / 425ºF / gas mark 7.

Peel the onion and slice very thinly. Heat the oil in a frying pan and cook the onions gently, until they are softened, and then allow them to brown and become slightly caramelised. This could take up to 25 minutes.

Cut the broccoli into florets and steam (or boil) quickly, until they are 'al dente' and retain a little crunch.

Roll out the pastry and divide into four equal rounds.

Break the cheese into pieces and mix with the mashed potato, add the cooked broccoli and onions, season to taste and mix well. The warm vegetables will begin to melt the cheese.

Place a portion of the mixture on one half of each of the pastry pieces.

Fold over the other half of the pastry to form a cover. Crimp the edges of the pastry to form a seal. Make a couple of small slits in the top of each pasty and brush with egg yolk and milk.

Place on a floured baking tray and bake for 25 minutes until the pastry has risen and golden.

Cornfed Chicken & Leek Pasty

A lovely taste of Wales here. The miners, when they could not afford chicken, often used sausage meat, and the Irish version of this recipe uses diced potatoes with strong onions in place of leeks.

450 g / 1 lb cornfed chicken meat, roughly chopped

50 g / 2 oz butter

4 leeks, cleaned and finely chopped

2 sprigs fresh parsley

3 tablespoons redcurrant jelly

225 g / 8 oz potatoes, cooked and diced

Salt and black pepper

450 g / 1 lb shortcrust pastry (see recipe on page 33)

1 egg, beaten with a little milk, to glaze

MAKES 6–8

Put the chicken meat into a frying pan with the butter, leeks and parsley, cover and cook for 25 minutes, stirring every five minutes.

Add the jelly and potatoes, seasoning well, and allow to cool.

Roll out the pastry to 5 mm / ¼ inch in thickness and cut out eight × 15 cm / 6 inch rounds.

Place the chicken mixture into the centre of each round, dampen the edges and fold them over to make a half-moon shape. Pinch and crimp the edges.

Glaze with the beaten egg mixture and put the pasties onto a greased baking sheet and bake at 180°C / 350°F / gas mark 4 for 35 minutes.

Serve with a crisp vegetable salad.

Try to use cornfed leg meat, which is more flavoursome and cheaper than the breast

The Ultimate Welsh Minced Lamb Pasty

15 ml / 1 tablespoon cooking oil

350 g / 12 oz extra lean minced Welsh lamb

1 small onion, finely diced

1 medium carrot, diced small

Salt and black pepper

1 medium potato, diced small

125 ml / 4½ fl oz lamb stock

1 egg yolk, beaten, to glaze

500 g / 1 lb 2 oz puff pastry (see recipe on page 39)

Flour for dusting

MAKES ABOUT 8

Pre-heat the oven to 200°C / 400°F / gas mark 6.

Heat the oil in a large saucepan, add the lamb and cook for 4 minutes until brown, then add the onion and carrot, cooking for a further 3 minutes. Add the lamb stock to the mince.

Put in the potatoes and simmer slowly for 30 minutes, adding more stock if needed. Season to taste then let the lamb mixture cool.

Roll out the puff pastry to about 5 mm / ¼ inch thick and cut it into about 8 squares.

Put about 25 g / 1 oz of the filling onto one half of each pastry square, but not to the edges. Brush the egg along the edge of one side of each pastry square and fold over. Crimp the edges, sealing well, and put a slit in top of each pasty to let steam out while cooking.

Brush egg over the top, place on a greased baking tray and cook in the oven for 25 minutes.

Bombay Potato Pasty

These simple spiced potato beauties are one of the most popular pasties I have ever made for friends and family. For a very special flavour use Jersey Royal potatoes when in season and serve in a puff or cheese pastry.

100 ml / 4 fl oz olive oil

1 teaspoon mustard seeds

¼ teaspoon of smoked chilli powder

¼ teaspoon saffron

Salt to taste

1 large red onion, finely chopped

30 ml / 2 tablespoons mild curry powder

450 g / 1 lb potatoes boiled and diced

450 g / 1 lb shortcrust pastry (see recipe on page 33)

MAKES 8

Heat the oil in a pan on a medium heat setting. To check that the oil is hot enough, sprinkle in a few mustard seeds, if they pop the oil is ready. Then add the remainder of the mustard seeds.

Add the chilli and saffron powders to the sizzling seeds, and salt to taste.

Fry this pungent mixture of oil and spices for 1 minute, add the onion and fry for 3 minutes, then add the potatoes and fry for about 4 minutes.

Add the curry powder, cook for a further 4 minutes until the potatoes are smothered in seeds and appear to have crispy edges. They will look quite yellow in colour. Cook now until they become very crisp, about a further 5 minutes. Let the potatoes rest for about 5 minutes.

Roll out the pastry to 5 mm / ¼ inch in thickness and cut out eight × 15 cm / 6 inch rounds.

Place the potato mixture into the centre of each round, dampen the edges of each round and fold them over to make a half-moon shape. Pinch and crimp the edges.

Glaze with the beaten egg, put the pasties onto a greased baking sheet and bake at 180°C / 350°F / gas mark 4 for 30 minutes.

The Fleetwood Fish Pasty

Fleetwood on the Lancashire coast, of course, is synonymous with fish, even though there is no longer a thriving fishing industry there. This recipe from the 1970s celebrates the port's heyday.

450 g / 1 lb brill fillets, skinned and chopped

450 g / 1 lb hake fillets, skinned and chopped

75 g / 3 oz plain, seasoned flour

Salt and black pepper

125 g / 5 oz butter

3 potatoes, diced

4 shallots, skinned and finely chopped

1 carrot, peeled and diced

1 leek, washed, and finely chopped

300 ml / ½ pint of fish stock

2 teaspoons anchovy essence

1 tablespoon tarragon vinegar

350 g / 12 oz uncooked tiger prawns, peeled and cleaned, tossed in lemon juice

150 ml / 5 fl oz cream

45 ml / 3 tablespoons freshly chopped parsley

1 kg / 2¼ lb cheese pastry (see recipe on page 41)

1 egg, beaten, to glaze

MAKES 10

Pre-heat the oven to 200°C / 400°F / gas mark 6.

Coat the fish in 25 g / 1 oz of the seasoned flour. Melt the butter in a large saucepan and add the fish, potatoes, shallots, carrot and leeks, cooking gently for 8 minutes. Sprinkle with the remaining flour, stirring for 2 minutes.

Slowly add the fish stock, anchovy essence and tarragon vinegar.

Keeping aside 10 tiger prawns, add the rest to the pan and simmer for 12 minutes on a low heat. Allow the mixture to cool, mix in the cream and parsley.

Roll out the cheese pastry to about 5 mm / ¼ inch thick and then cut it into about 10 squares.

Put about 35–45 g / 1–2 oz onto one side of pastry and top with a raw tiger prawn, brush the egg round the edges of each pastry square and fold over. Crimp the edges and put a slit in the top to let steam out while cooking.

Brush egg over the top and place on greased baking tray and cook in the centre of the oven for 25 minutes.

Accompaniments

There is nothing nicer when serving a hotpot, picnic pie or pasty than being able to offer homemade piccalilli, beetroot, red cabbage etc. So to finish this fun cookbook I give you some interesting recipes from yesteryear that are far better – and purer – than most of the mass-produced stuff that populates our supermarket shelves.

When potting preserves make sure the jars – properly sterilised – are clean, dry and warm. Fill the jars to the brim with the HOT finished preserve or jelly and cover with a round of greaseproof paper. Use plastic-coated twist tops (the ones with the clickable button if re-using jars) or kilner jars, and seal while the preserves are hot. Label and date each jar and store in a dry, cool and dark area. Most preserves will keep for up to 12 months, but do check before eating if you've had it a while, and always keep opened jars in the fridge.

Mrs Beeton's pickled red cabbage (1861)

Red cabbage

Salt

Water

1.2 litre / 2 pints vinegar – to each quart add 1 tablespoon ginger, well bruised

25 g / 1 oz whole black pepper

A little cayenne, if liked

Take off the outside decayed leaves of a nice red cabbage, cut it into quarters, remove the stalks, and cut it across in very thin slices.

Lay these in a dish, and cover them plentifully with salt, then cover with another dish.

Leave for 24 hours; turn into a colander to drain, and if necessary, wipe lightly with a clean, soft cloth. Put them in a jar; boil up the vinegar with the spices, and when cold, pour it over the cabbage. It will be fit for use in a week or two, but if kept for a very long time, the cabbage is liable to get soft and discoloured. To be really nice and crisp, and of a good red colour, it should be eaten almost immediately after it is made. A little bruised cochineal boiled with the vinegar adds greatly to the appearance of this pickle. Tie down with bladder, and keep in a dry place.

Victorian piccalilli

You could walk into most homes in the 1960s and see a jar of piccalilli on the dining table or in the cupboard. This sunny pickle was a simple and effective way of using up the end of season vegetables in a way that meant we could have them out of season. Today, of course, we can get most vegetables all year round, but it's still a great little accompaniment to so many dishes.

450 g / 1 lb cauliflower, cut into small florets

450 g / 1 lb small pickling onions, peeled

1.2 litres / 2 pints malt vinegar

½ whole nutmeg freshly grated

3 ml / ¾ teaspoon powdered allspice

1 large cucumber, de-seed and cut into rounds with a ½ cm ball scoop

100 g / 4 oz caster sugar

75 g / 3 oz English mustard powder

90 g / 3½ oz plain flour

35 g / 1½ oz turmeric powder

Salt and white pepper

Place the cauliflower florets, onions and vinegar together in a large saucepan. Add the nutmeg and allspice and bring gently to the boil, cover and simmer for 6 minutes. Take the lid from the pan and add the cucumber and sugar. Simmer again for a further 3 minutes.

Place a colander over a large bowl and carefully pour the contents into the colander. Leave the vegetables to drain and then reserve the vinegar.

Place the mustard powder, flour and turmeric into a separate bowl, add 60 ml / 4 tablespoons of the reserved vinegar and blend to a fine paste. Add a ladle of the vinegar and blend thoroughly and transfer to a saucepan, slowly bring to the boil, whisking vigorously, slowly adding the remaining vinegar. Boil gently for 6 minutes and place the vegetables into a large bowl, season them well with salt and pepper.

Pour the mustard sauce over the vegetables. Stir well, and then carefully spoon the mixture into heated, warmed and dried screw-top jars. Keep for at least a month before eating with hot or cold pies and pasties.

To de-seed the cucumber, cut it lengthways and with a dessert spoon scoop out the central pulp until all you have left is the outer green shell, which you cut into small dice

Yorkshire relish

One of the oldest preserve recipes in Yorkshire history. The story goes that when eating in coachhouses and inns a Yorkshireman would become very suspicious if meat was covered with gravy, thinking that it was yesterday's leftovers warmed and tarted up! So they would ask for cold beef with a sauce boat of Yorkshire relish so they could see exactly what they were getting! Served with the growler, game or meat and potato pies this relish is excellent.

600 ml / 1 pint malt vinegar

100 g / 4 oz soft brown sugar

1 teaspoon of salt

6 black peppercorns

25 g / 1 oz chopped chillies

1 tablespoon black treacle

1 tablespoon Worcestershire sauce

1 tablespoon mushroom ketchup

½ teaspoon freshly grated nutmeg

Place all the ingredients into a saucepan and bring slowly to the boil, simmering for 10 minutes.

Allow the mixture to cool then pour into warm clean bottles or jars with cork or vinegar-proof tops.

This relish will keep for about 18 months if stored in a dry, dark place and will mature with age.

Rhubarb chutney

A must with any pie, hot or cold, and a summer favourite in my family.

450 g / 1 lb rhubarb (red end),
    washed and chopped

2 onions, chopped

3 tablespoons sultanas

2 tablespoons soft brown sugar

Pinch of cayenne pepper

1 teaspoon English mustard
    powder

1 teaspoon salt

1 tablespoon mild curry paste

2 tablespoons of port

150 ml / ¼ pint white wine
    vinegar

Put all the ingredients into a large saucepan, bring to the boil and simmer slowly for 10 minutes, stirring all the time. Boil rapidly for a further 3 minutes until the rhubarb is fully cooked.

Put into warm jars and seal. Let it stand for 7 days before using.

I once saw a Chinese pickled egg sold at an auction for £1,000, and the person who bought it proceeded to eat it there and then – no bread, no cheese, nothing; some people have no etiquette!

Pickled eggs

The eggs should be boiled for 10 minutes, stirring them after the first 3 minutes to centralise the yolks. Then plunge them into cold water for 12 minutes.

12 fresh eggs, hard boiled and
    shelled

600 ml / 1 pint white wine
    vinegar

3 blades of mace

Pack the eggs into glass jars and cover with the vinegar, adding a blade of mace to each jar.

Seal and leave for 1 month before using.

Raspberry vinegar

This is a really refreshing dressing for all summer salads, and it goes especially well with cold pork pies and a beetroot salad.

900 g / 2 lb fresh raspberries
2 litre white wine vinegar
900 g / 2 lb granulated sugar

Put the hulled raspberries into a large clean glass bowl. Pour over enough vinegar to cover the raspberries. Cover and leave them to stand for 4 days, stirring every day.

Strain the liquid, not the raspberries, through a non-metallic sieve, being very careful not to crush the raspberries through the sieve as this will make the vinegar cloudy. Pour the juices into a saucepan, add the sugar, bring the juice to the boil and then simmer for 20 minutes.

Let the liquid stand until it is completely cold and then bottle and seal using vinegar-proof tops. Let it stand for at least 4 days before use.

You can use this same recipe and method with any soft fruit berries.

Red cabbage

You can serve this with almost any savoury dish but I reckon it should always be offered with hashes and hotpots. Choose a really firm cabbage, removing any discoloured leaves, and before shredding cut it into quarters, taking out the inner stalk.

1 red cabbage, washed and shredded

100 g / 4 oz cooking salt

50 g / 2 oz soft brown sugar

600 ml / 1 pint white wine vinegar

Place the shredded cabbage, salt and sugar in layers in a large basin, cover with cling film and leave it to stand for 24 hours.

Rinse the cabbage in cold water, draining it well. Pack the cabbage quite loosely into jars and cover with the white wine vinegar and seal with vinegar-proof tops.

Let the mixture stand for at least 7 days before using and use within 3 months or it will lose its crispness.

Pickled onions

I make my pickled onions quite sweet and I also use milder vinegar than spiced or pickling vinegar. I find white wine vinegar less tangy and the use of soft brown sugar mellows the sharpness of the pickles.

To make spiced vinegar put 8 cloves, 12 g / ½ oz pieces of ginger and cinnamon, and 8 white peppercorns into 1 litre of malt vinegar. Bottle for 2 months and shake every week. Strain and use when required.

900 g / 2 lb pickling onions, peeled

600 ml / 20 fl oz spiced or pickling vinegar, hot but not boiling

100 g / 4 oz soft brown sugar

12 g / ½ oz salt

5 g / 1 teaspoon of pink peppercorns

Put all the ingredients into a glass bowl, stir with a wooden spoon until the sugar dissolves.

Pack the pickles into jars and top up with the vinegar, seal with vinegar-proof tops (plastic-coated, or glass, as with kilner jars) and leave them to stand for at least 4 to 6 weeks before using them.

Tom's beetroot 'caviar'

No sugar needs be added here because the natural sweetness of the beetroot is enough. It is quite important to use a very high quality aged balsamic syrup and virgin olive oil.

2 × 250 g packs cooked beetroot

1 large red onion, very finely chopped

60 ml / 4 tablespoons extra virgin olive oil

60 ml / 4 tablespoons aged balsamic syrup

Salt and black pepper

Dice the beetroot extremely finely and combine all the ingredients.

Place into an airtight container and chill for 24 hours. The beetroot caviar is now ready to serve with any summer salad.

This is excellent served with a picnic pie or ploughman's lunch

Rowan jelly

The rowan berries must be just ripe and the apples sweet and fresh for this recipe. Serve with game pie, venison pasties and pork pies. I use fresh apple juice instead of water for a real crisp flavour.

900 g / 2 lb rowan berries

900 g / 2 lb Cox's Orange Pippin

Apple juice to cover

2 kg / 4½ lb sugar with pectin

Remove any stalks from the rowan berries, wash and drain them.

Peel, core and chop the apples.

Place the fruits into a large saucepan and just cover with apple juice. Cook for 15 minutes then strain the fruit and liquid through a fine sieve into another clean saucepan. Add the sugar and pectin. Boil rapidly for 15 minutes until the jelly is nearly at setting point, then pot and seal in warm jars.

Mint sauce

It is very important that very good quality wine vinegar is used when making mint sauce. Perfect served with my mutton and lamb pies.

45 ml / 3 tablespoons of finely chopped mint

15 ml / 1 tablespoon caster sugar

15 ml / 1 tablespoon boiling water

30 ml / 2 tablespoons wine vinegar

Put the leaves into a sauce boat with the sugar, add the boiling water and allow to cool. Add the vinegar and allow it to infuse for at least one hour before serving.

Cranberry sauce

For pork, chicken and turkey.

450 g / 1 lb fresh cranberries
(washed)
300 ml / ½ pint water
100 g / 4 oz brown sugar

Stew the Cranberries in the water until they 'pop'. Rub them through a fine sieve.

Sweeten with the brown sugar and reheat. It is ready to serve immediately, or you can pot it in jars and seal while still hot.

Try honey instead of sugar for a slightly different taste

Gooseberry sauce

This classic sauce dates back to the seventeenth century when it was – and indeed still is – served with mackerel. Try this with my stargazy pie, or any other strongly flavoured fish pie or pasty.

225 g / 8 oz green gooseberries
150 ml / ¼ pint water
25 g / 1 oz butter
25 g / 1 oz sugar
Juice of 1 lemon
Freshly grated nutmeg
Salt and black pepper

Slowly stew the gooseberries very gently with the water and butter until they are pulpy then turn off the heat. Beat them with a wire whisk until they are smooth.

Reheat the sauce, stir in the sugar, lemon juice and a little grated nutmeg to taste. Add a few chives or some sorrel if you desire.

For a stronger sauce use fish stock instead of water

Currant sauce

This is a nineteenth-century recipe for a sauce that goes particularly well with venison, rabbit and game pies.

50 g / 2 oz dried currants
25 g / 1 oz butter
25 g / 1 oz flour
300 ml / ½ pint chicken stock
15 ml / 1 tablespoon brown
    sugar
150 ml / ¼ pint white wine
15 ml / 1 tablespoon white wine
    vinegar
Rind and juice of 1 lemon
A little freshly grated nutmeg
Pinch of ground cloves
A little freshly grated root
    ginger

Melt the butter and cook the currants for 1 minute, blend in the flour and cook for 4 minutes.

Add the stock and simmer for 5 minutes. Add the rest of the ingredients bring to the boil and simmer on a low heat for 20 minutes, stirring all the time.

Try using sultanas instead of currants

Redcurrant sauce

Heat 100 g / 4 oz redcurrant jelly and 60 ml / 4 tablespoons port in a saucepan and cook gently for 3 minutes. Serve with any game pie.

Apple sauce

Heavenly with pork or cheese pies.

450 g / 1 lb Bramley apples,
  peeled, cored and chopped

30 ml / 2 tablespoons water

12 g / ½ oz butter

30 ml / 2 tablespoons castor
  sugar

5 ml / 1 teaspoon tarragon
  vinegar

Pinch of ground cloves

Melt the butter in a saucepan, add the chopped apple with the water, cover and cook gently for 8 minutes.

Remove the pan from the heat and mash the apples to a soft, smooth mixture. Stir in the sugar, vinegar and cloves.

Re-heat, stirring all the time and place into a sauceboat.

Beetroot & apple salad with English dressing

A marriage made in heaven for the pork pie.

For the dressing

1 tablespoon English mustard
  powder

2 teaspoons honey

50 ml / 3 tablespoons raspberry
  vinegar
  (see recipe on page 240

Salt and black pepper

150–175 ml / 5–6 fl oz quality
  olive oil

Mixture

4 cooked beetroot cut into
  wedges

3 Cox's Orange pippin apples

2 pineapple rings (optional)

1 carrot

1 large sprig parsley

115 ml / 4½ fl oz English
  dressing

2 tablespoons sesame seeds

Mix together mustard, honey, wine vinegar and seasoning.

Whisk in olive oil until you get an emulsified dressing.

Place the sesame seeds in a heavy bottomed frying pan (without oil) over a low to medium heat and toast until golden brown, being sure not to allow them to burn by shaking the pan all the time.

Wash, core and slice the apples into thin wedges.

Peel and coarsely grate the carrot.

If using the pineapple cut it into small wedges.

Wash, drain and finely chop the parsley.

Place all of the ingredients in a bowl, pouring over the dressing, mix thoroughly to ensure everything is well coated.

Beetroot, carrot, parsnip & sweet potato crisps

Vegetable crisps are a wonderful accompaniment to any cold pie and salad. They cost an absolute fortune in food stores but they are so easy to make at home. If placed in an air-tight container they will stay fresh and crisp for weeks.

Rapeseed or vegetable oil for deep frying

6 parsnips, peeled

2 large sweet potatoes, peeled

4 large carrots, peeled

4 large raw beetroots, peeled

Salt and black pepper

Pre-heat a deep fat fryer to 190°C / 375°F.

Thinly slice the parsnips, carrots, sweet potatoes and beetroot (keeping them separate) using a vegetable peeler, sharp knife or mandolin.

Working in batches, deep-fry the parsnips, carrots, sweet potatoes and then the beetroots for 2 minutes each until crisp. Drain on kitchen paper and season well. Place into a presentation serving dish, tossing the three types of crisps together carefully and if you are serving at once, season with salt and pepper. Alternatively, you can store them in an airtight container.

Apricot & cranberry stuffing

75 g / 3 oz butter

2 onions, finely chopped

75 g / 3 oz fresh cranberries

1 tablespoon lemon juice and zest

75 g / 3 oz dried apricots diced

450 g / 1 lb dried breadcrumbs

¾ teaspoon dried thyme

1 teaspoon chopped parsley

Salt and black pepper

150 ml / ¼ pint chicken stock

75 ml / 3 fl oz apple juice

Melt the butter in a large saucepan, add the onions and cook gently until the onions have softened, about 5 minutes. Remove from the heat and allow to cool. Add all the rest of the ingredients into the saucepan and mix. Cook slowly for 12 minutes. Taste for more seasoning and place to one side until required.

This stuffing is wonderful on sandwiches with leftover roast pork, chicken, turkey and naturally smoked ham.

Handmade curry powder & a curry sauce from an Englishman!

First you need a very good curry powder, and I suggest you make your own to this traditional recipe.

75 g / 3 oz coriander seed

75 g / 3 oz turmeric

5 whole cloves

25 g / 1 oz each of: black pepper, mustard powder, ginger, allspice, cardamoms, cayenne, cumin seeds and garlic powder

Thoroughly pound all the spice ingredients together and use it when required.

Curry sauce

50 g / 2 oz butter

100 g / 4 oz finely sliced onion

15 ml / 1 tablespoon of curry powder

25 g / 1 oz flour

1 garlic clove crushed

10 g / ½ oz tomato puree

375 ml / ¾ pint of chicken stock

25 g / 1 oz chopped apple

25 g / 1 oz sultanas and raisins

160 ml / 6 fl oz coconut milk

Salt and black pepper

A little natural yoghurt or soured cream

In a large saucepan melt the butter and gently cook the onion and crushed garlic. Mix in the curry powder and the flour, cooking gently for 5 minutes. Add the tomato puree and the stock to make a smooth sauce. Add the apple, sultanas and raisins and season with salt and pepper, simmering for at least 40 minutes.

Stir in the coconut milk. Should you feel that it is too strong, then add a little natural yoghurt or soured cream.

This is a highly spiced sauce which was prepared in England as long ago as the reign of King Richard II – two 'receipts' for curry powders are given in the roll compiled by his master cooks about the year 1390.

But the greatest authority on curries and curry-making is Dr William Kitchiner, and I base my sauce on his wonderful recipe of 1813 – copied, quite openly by Mrs Beeton in her Book of Household Management in 1861.

Conversion tables

All these are approximate conversions, which have either been rounded up or down. In a few recipes, it has been necessary to modify them very slightly.

Never mix metric and imperial measures in one recipe; stick to one system or the other.

All spoon measurements are level, unless specified otherwise.

All butter is salted, unless specified otherwise.

All recipes are tested using whole milk, unless specified otherwise.

American Cup Conversions

American	Metric	Imperial
1 cup flour	150 g	5 oz
1 cup caster and granulated sugar	225 g	8 oz
1 cup brown sugar	175 g	6 oz
1 cup butter / margarine / lard	225 g	8 oz
1 cup sultanas / raisins	200 g	7 oz
1 cup currants	150 g	5 oz
1 cup ground almonds	110 g	4 oz
1 cup golden syrup	350 g	12 oz
1 cup uncooked rice	200 g	7 oz
1 cup grated cheese	110 g	4 oz
1 stick butter	110 g	4 oz

Liquid Conversions

American	Metric	Imperial
1 teaspoon	5 ml	1 teaspoon
½ fl oz	15 ml	1 tablespoon
¼ cup	60 ml	4 tablespoons
½ cup plus 2 tablespoons	150 ml	¼ pint
1¼ cups	275 ml	½ pint
1 pint / 16 fl oz	450 ml	¾ pint
2½ pints / 5 cups	1.4 litres	2 pints
10 pints	4.8 litres	8 pints

Weights

Metric	Imperial	Metric	Imperial	Metric	Imperial	Metric	Imperial
10 g	½ oz	75 g	3 oz	200 g	7 oz	350 g	12 oz
20 g	¾ oz	110 g	4 oz	225 g	8 oz	450 g	1 lb
25 g	1 oz	125 g	4½ oz	250 g	9 oz	700 g	1 lb 8 oz
40 g	1½ oz	150 g	5 oz	275 g	10 oz	900 g	2 lb
50 g	2 oz	175 g	6 oz	300 g	11 oz	1.35 kg	3 lb
60 g	2½ oz						

Dimensions

Metric	Imperial
3 mm	⅛ inch
5 mm	¼ inch
1 cm	½ inch
2 cm	¾ inch
2.5 cm	1 inch
3 cm	1¼ inch
4 cm	1½ inch

Metric	Imperial
4.5 cm	1¾ inch
5 cm	2 inch
6 cm	2½ inch
7.5 cm	3 inch
9 cm	3½ inch
10 cm	4 inch
13 cm	5 inch

Metric	Imperial
13.5 cm	5¼ inch
15 cm	6 inch
16 cm	6½ inch
18 cm	7 inch
19 cm	7½ inch
20 cm	8 inch
23 cm	9 inch

Metric	Imperial
24 cm	9½ inch
25.5 cm	10 inch
28 cm	11 inch
30 cm	12 inch

Volume

Metric	Imperial	
5 ml		1 teaspoon
15 ml	½ fl oz	1 tablespoon
30 ml	1 fl oz	2 tablespoons
55 ml	2 fl oz	
60 ml		4 tablespoons
75 ml	3 fl oz	
80 ml	3½ fl oz	5 tablespoons
150 ml	5 fl oz (¼ pint)	
200 ml	7 fl oz	
250 ml	8 fl oz	

Metric	Imperial
275 ml	10 fl oz (½ pint)
600 ml	1 pint
725 ml	1¼ pint
1 litre	1¾ pint
1.2 litre	2 pint
1.4 litre	2½ pint
1.75 litres	3 pint
2 lites	3½ pint
2.25 litre	4 pint

Oven Temperatures

°C	°F	gas mark
140°C	275°F	1
150°C	300°F	2
170°C	325°F	3
180°C	350°F	4
190°C	375°F	5

°C	°F	gas mark
200°C	400°F	6
220°C	425°F	7
230°C	450°F	8
240°C	475°F	9

Bibliography

Aylett, Mary and Olive Ordish, *First Catch Your Hare* (1965: Macdonald & Co.)

Acton, Eliza, *Modern Cooking in All its Branches* (1845: Longman, Brown & Green)

Beeton, Isabella, *The Book of Household Management* (1861: S.O.Beeton)

Bridge, Tom, *The People of Bolton on Cookery* (1982: self published, Tom Bridge)

Bridge, Tom, *The Golden Age of Cookery* (1983: Ross Anderson)

Bridge, Tom and Colin Cooper English, *Dr William Kitchiner – Regency Eccentric, Author of the Cooks Oracle (*1992: Southover Press)

Bridge, Tom, *200 Classic Sauces* (1995: Cassell)

Bridge, Tom, *Bridge Over Britain* (1996: Cassell)

Bridge, Tom, *Bridge On British Beef* (1997: Piatkus)

Bridge, Tom, *What's Cooking Chicken* (1999: Paragon)

Bridge, Tom, *The Golden Age of Food* (1999: Waterton)

Bridge, Tom, *The Ultimate Game Cookbook* (1999: Piatkus)

Bridge, Tom, *Classic Recipes from Scotland* (2005: Mainstream)

Colquhoun, Kate, *Taste: The Story of Britain through its Cooking* (2008: Bloomsbury)

Dods, Margaret, *The Cook and Housewife's Manual* (1826: Edinburgh)

Escoffier, Auguste, *Guide to Modern Cookery* (1907: Heineman)

Pegge, Samuel, *A Forme of Cury* (1390) (1780: J. Nicholls)

Francatelli, Charles Elme, *The Cook's Guide* (1869: Richard Bentley)

Glasse, Hannah, *The Art of Cookery Made Plain and Easy, By a Lady* (1747: London)

Graig, Elizabeth, *New Standard Cookery* (1932: Odhams Press)

Hartley Dorothy, *Food in England* (1954: Macdonald & Co.)

Hix, Mark , *British Regional Food* (2008: Quadrille)

Hutchins, Sheila, *English Recipes and Others* (1967: Methuen & Co.)

Jewry, Mary, *Warne's Model Cookery and Housekeeping Book* (1868: Fredrick Warne)

Kitchiner, Dr William, *The Cook's Oracle* (1817: London)

Marshall, Agnes.B, *Mrs A.B.Marshall's Cookery Book* (1888: Simkin & Marshall)

McNeill, Marian, T*he Scots Kitchen – Its Lore and Recipes* (1929: Blackie)

Raffald, Elizabeth, *The Experienced English House-keeper* (1769: J.Harrop)

Rundle Mrs, *New System of Domestic Cookery* (1807: John Murray)

Unknown, *The Young Woman's Companion or Frugal Housewife* (1813: Russell & Allen)

White, Florence, *Good Things in England* (1932: Jonathan Cape)

Index of Recipes

Acknowledgements

I would like to thank everyone from the British savoury pie, pasty and pudding industry who has contributed to this book, especially the following: Samworth Brothers; Larry File at Ginsters; Stephen Hallam of Dickinson & Morris; Richard Earl of Bradford and everyone at Porters Restaurant in Covent Garden; Sally Voss, Andrew and Tim Storer at Pukka Pies; John Green and the team at Wilsons in Leeds; the Mutton Renaissance; John and family at Carrs Pasties, Bolton; Marie Walsh and all the staff at Ye Olde Pastie Shoppe in Bolton; Sean Horton at Goddard's Pies, the only pie & mash shop in Great Britain; John Spencer at the Cheddar Gorge Cheese Company; Shirley Roberts, who makes some of the most wonderful pies ever in Lancashire; Russell Walsh at Potts Pies, who keeps Morecambe fans FC fed; Janet Purcell at Denby Dale Pie Co; Ann Muller in Cornwall and all the pasty shops around that coastline; John Fallon at Grants Haggis; Laura Medel and Magdalena Kobylinska at Geometry PR; Claire Bradley at HD Communications.

My gratitude also goes to chefs Mark Hix, Alan Bird, Brian Turner, Andrew Nutter, Anthony Worrall Thompson, Hugh Fearnley-Whittingstall, Robert Owen Brown and Domenico Crolla.

Big hugs to my partner in pie crime, television producer and all round good egg Nichola Dixon. And thanks too to TV presenters Jilly Goolden, Mel Giedroyc, Sue Perkins and Fred Talbot.

I can't thank Simon Mason at Axis Digital Photography enough for his friendship and expertise in photographing my dishes and making food look normal, not airbrushed. This book would not look half as good as it does without his photographs, which are easy to spot as they are usually the best ones – if a picture looks amateurish it's probably mine, Simon's are all top quality! (Visit www.axis-digital-photography.com for more information.)

I would also particularly like to thank my dear friend Richard Russum (www.russams.co.uk), who has supported all my cookbooks and supplied me with my chef whites and equipment when I needed it. Thanks Richard.

A special thank you to Jackie, Philippa, Eileen; Carl Gibney and all his staff at Choice Cuts; Ken Longworth; John Bates Fruit & Veg; and all the staff at Salmon King on Bolton Market; PC genius Scott Wilson; Ernie and Sandra Clark (Wiganers); Becky Want at BBC Radio Manchester; Peter Smith; Nicky and Tracey Dowson; Pippa and Mo Hardy; Dave Cross; all at BBC1 and BBC2 and all at Love Productions in London.

And not forgetting Said Durra and his production team at Premier League Productions in London for his enthusiasm on the terraces; Geoff Wood and everyone in the KORB Ballykinler, Northern Ireland – never forgotten; Anna Goddard, Lucy Frontani and all the team at Carnegie Publishing Ltd for having faith in my work and producing such a lovely book so quickly! My family, Jayne Ellis Bridge, Matt and Gaz.

Finally, to anyone else involved with this mouth watering book that I might have missed out, I did not mean to and your help was greatly appreciated.

Thank you all!